Name:

Print Child's Name

Kick Start Kindergarten

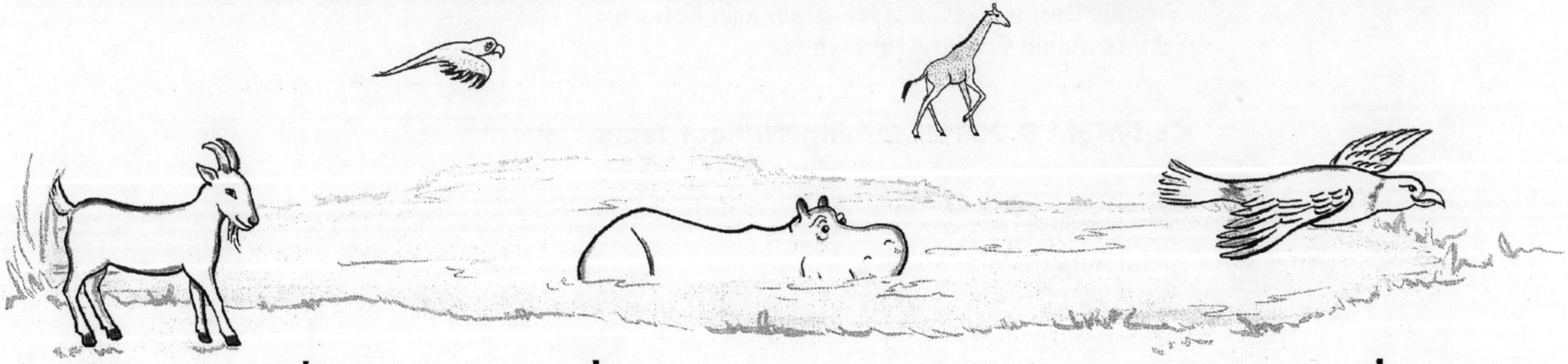

goat hippo eagle

8001 MacArthur Blvd
Cabin John, MD 20818
LWTears.com | 888.983.8409

Author: Jan Z. Olsen, OTR
Content Advisors: Christina Bretz, OTR/L, Tania Ferrandino, OTR/L, Robert Walnock, M.Ed.
Illustrators: Jan Z. Olsen, OTR, Julie Koborg
Graphic Designers: Carol Johnston, Julie Koborg
Editors: Annie Cassidy, Kathryn Fox

Second Edition
ISBN: 978-1-939814-43-2
123456789RPR212019
Printed in the USA

Dear Friend,

It's time for letters.

It's time for numbers.

It's time to color, too.

This book is for you!

Jan Z. Olsen

A B C D E F G H I J K L M N O P Q R S T U V W X Y Z

31 11 26 9 8 7 29 16 32 34 17 18 14 13 27 10 28 12 30 33 19 20 21 22 23 24

TABLE OF CONTENTS

Getting Started

Capitals

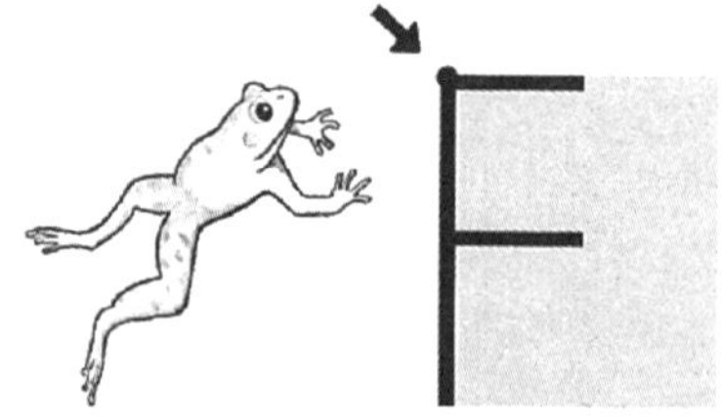

Frog Jump Capitals

Teach numbers with capitals.

See teaching guidelines in the teacher's guide.

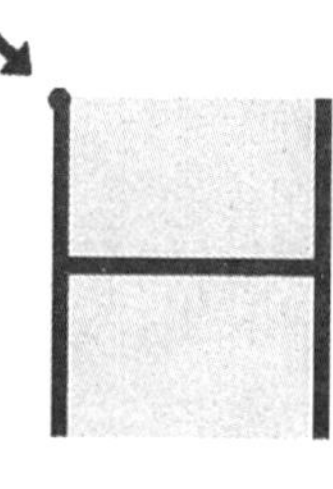

Starting Corner Capitals

Center Starting Capitals

Numbers

Lowercase Letters

Same as Capitals and t

Magic c Letters

More Vowels

Transition Group

Diver Letters

Final Group

CAPITALS

All are tall.
All start at the top.

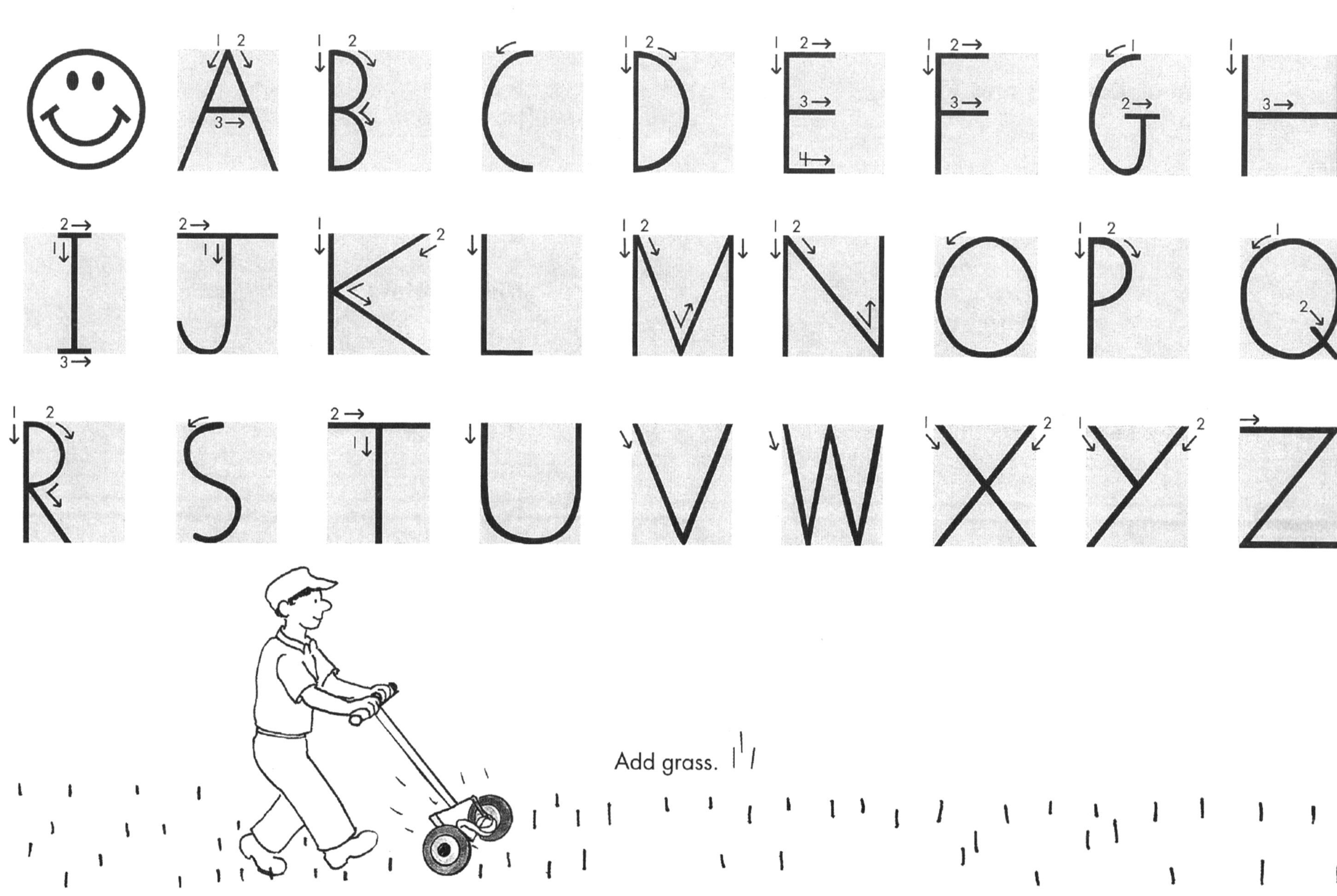

Add grass.

Help Me Write My Name

Make shining stars.
Trace and add swirls.

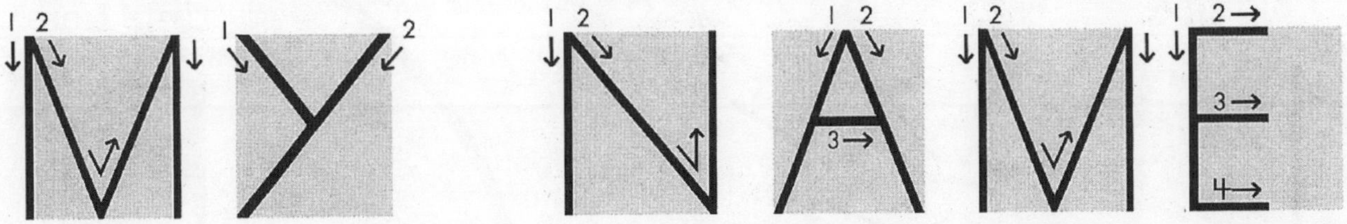

MY NAME

Teacher demonstrates.
Child copies below.

FROG JUMP CAPITALS

F E D P B R N M are the Frog Jump Capitals.

Frog Jump Capitals start in the Starting Corner on the dot.
Make a Big Line down.
Frog Jump back to the Starting Corner.
Now you are ready to finish the letter.

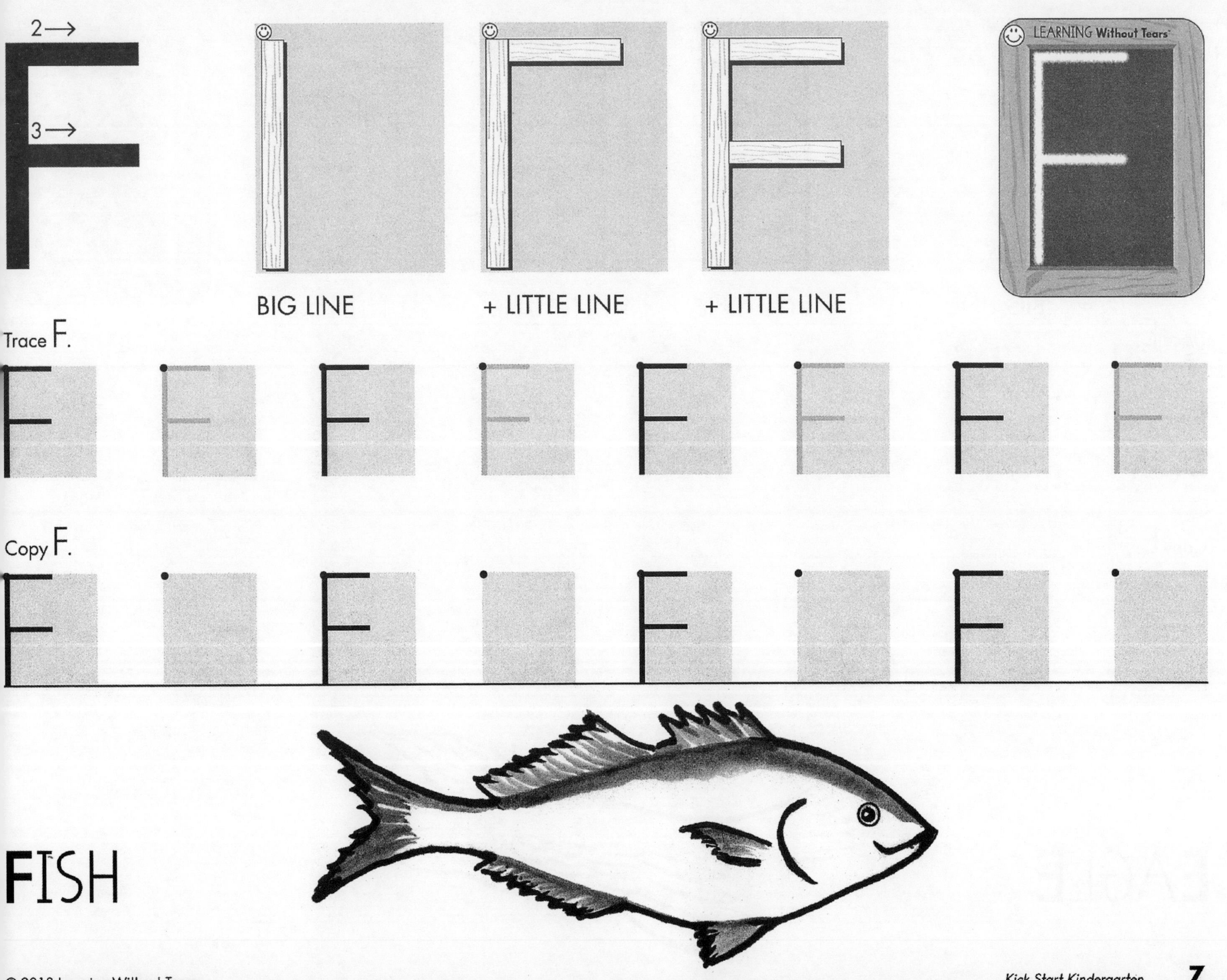
2→
3→
BIG LINE
+ LITTLE LINE
+ LITTLE LINE
LEARNING Without Tears
Trace F.
Copy F.
FISH

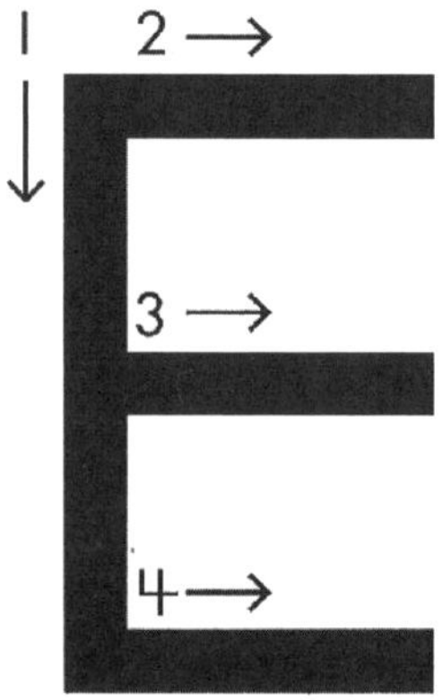

1 2 → 3 → 4 →

E

BIG LINE + LITTLE LINE + LITTLE LINE + LITTLE LINE

LEARNING Without Tears

Trace E.

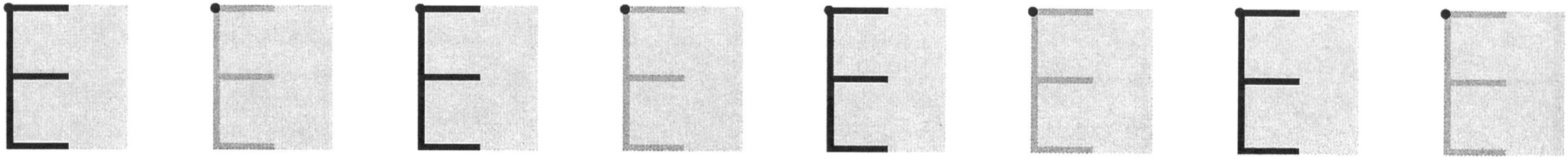

E E E E E E E E

Copy E.

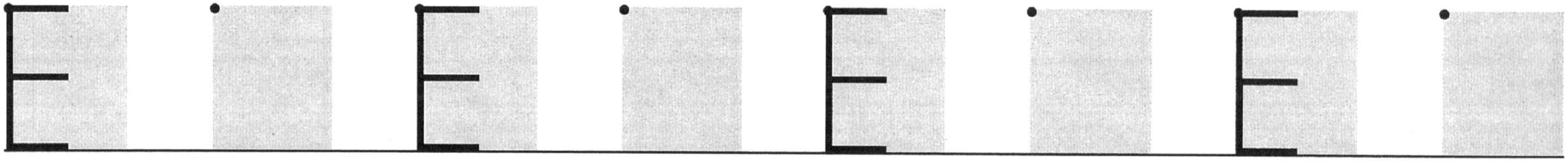

E E E E

EAGLE

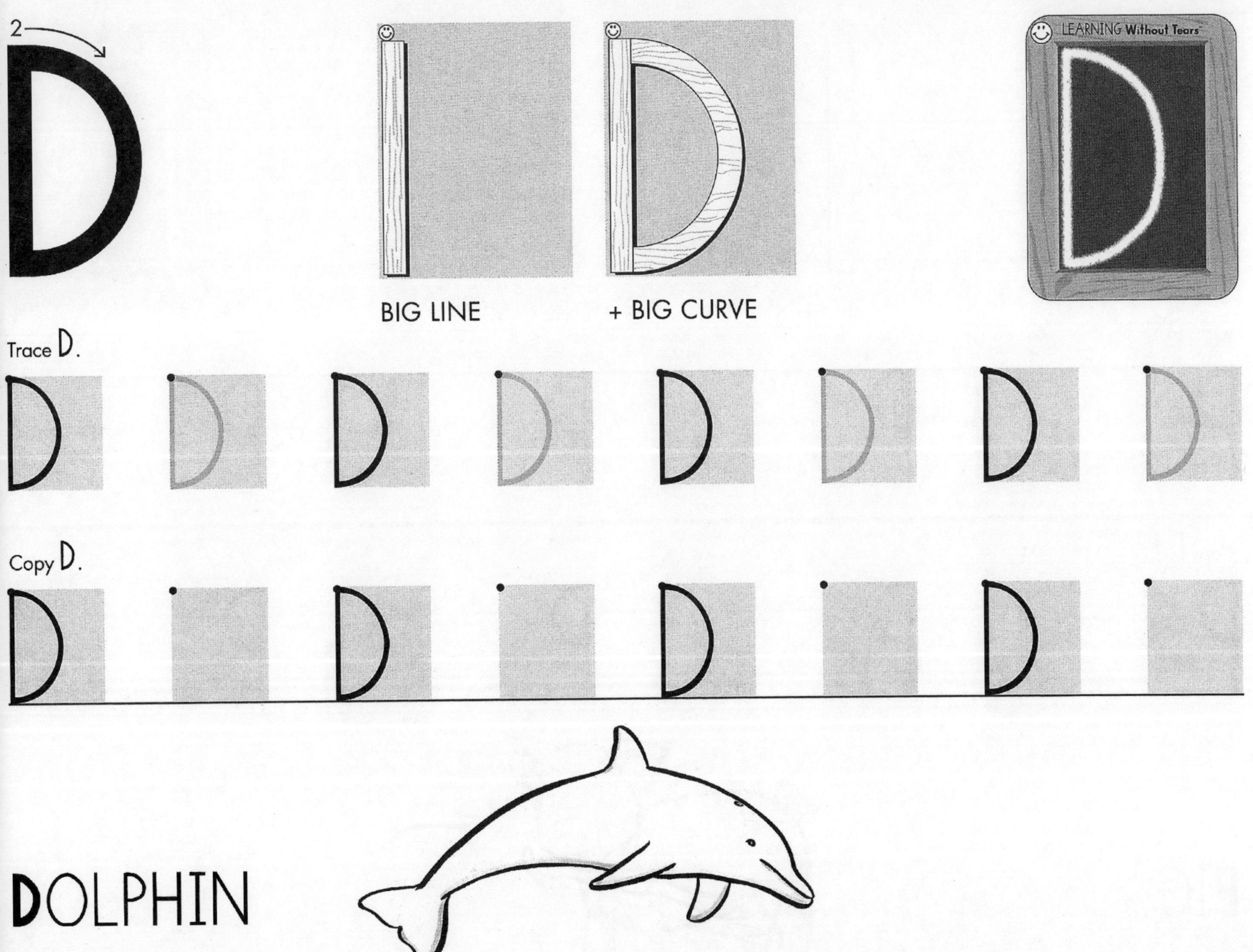

2
LEARNING Without Tears
BIG LINE
+ BIG CURVE
Trace D.
Copy D.
DOLPHIN

1 2

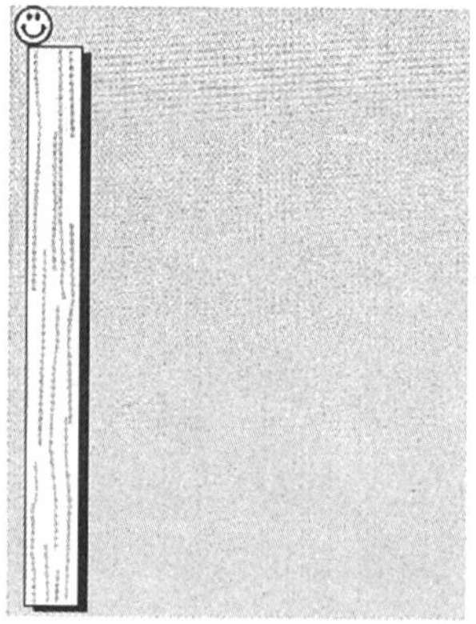

P

BIG LINE 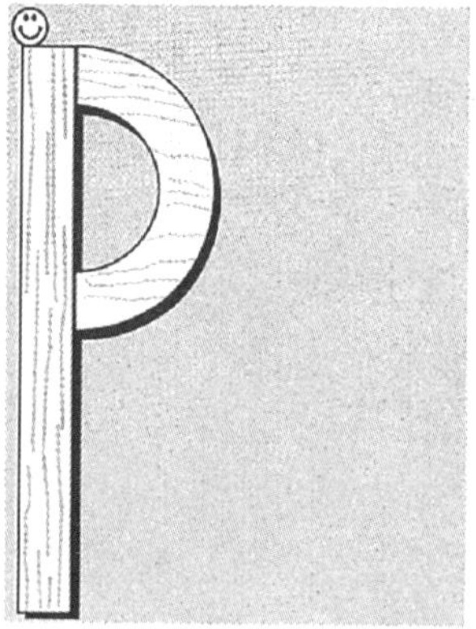 + LITTLE CURVE

LEARNING Without Tears

Trace P.

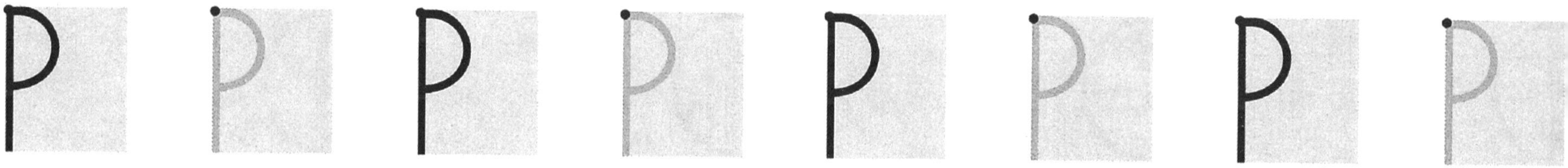

Copy P.

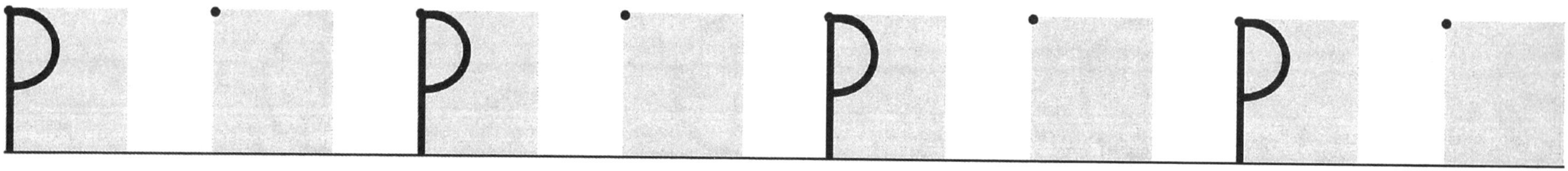

PIG

2
B
LEARNING Without Tears
BIG LINE
+ LITTLE CURVE
+ LITTLE CURVE
Trace B.
Copy B.
BED

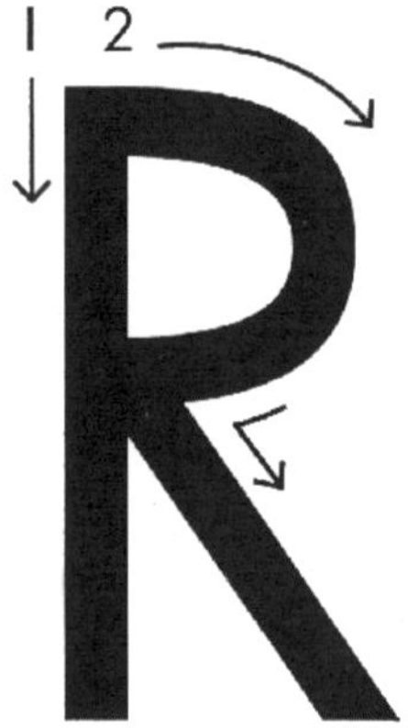

1 2

R

BIG LINE

+ LITTLE CURVE

+ LITTLE LINE

LEARNING Without Tears

R

Trace R.

R R R R R R R R

Copy R.

R R R R

RAINBOW

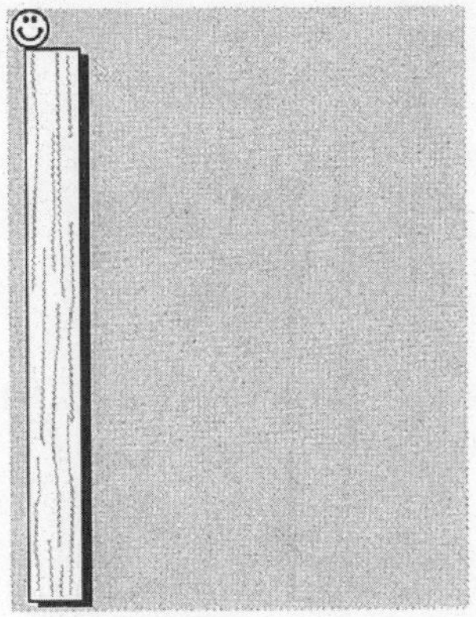

N

BIG LINE

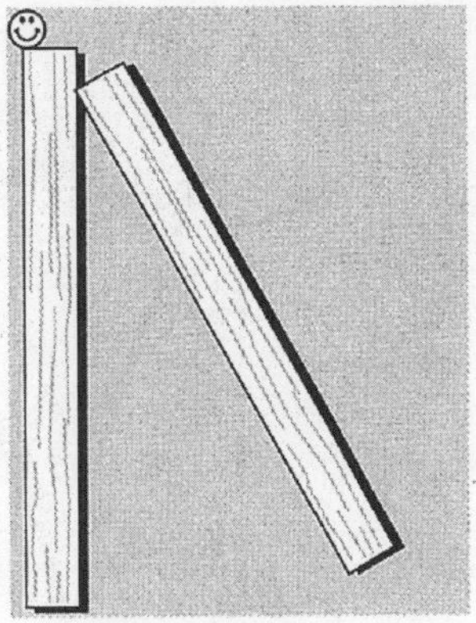

+ BIG LINE

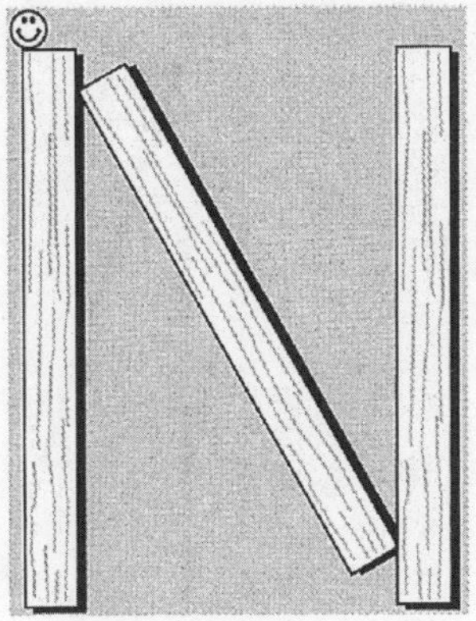

+ BIG LINE

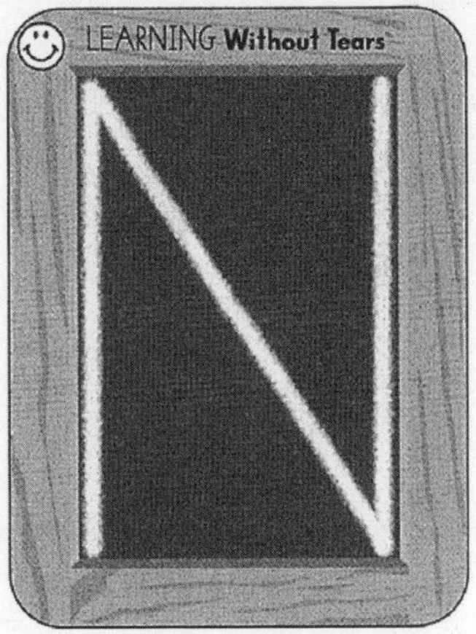

LEARNING Without Tears

Trace N.

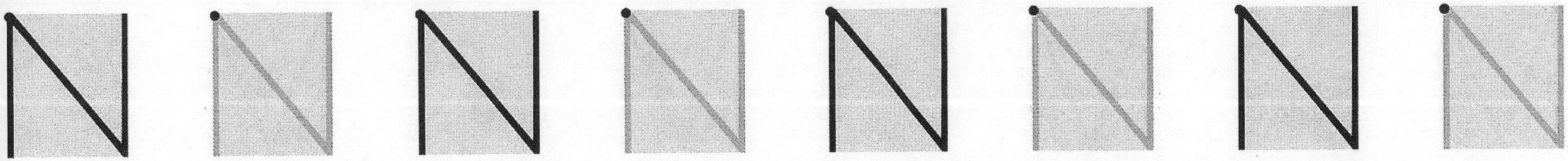

Copy N.

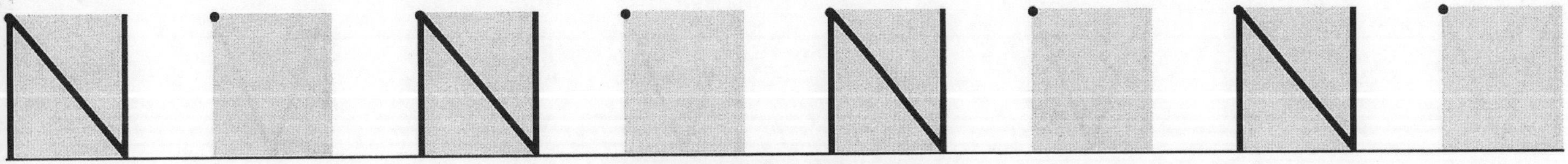

NEST

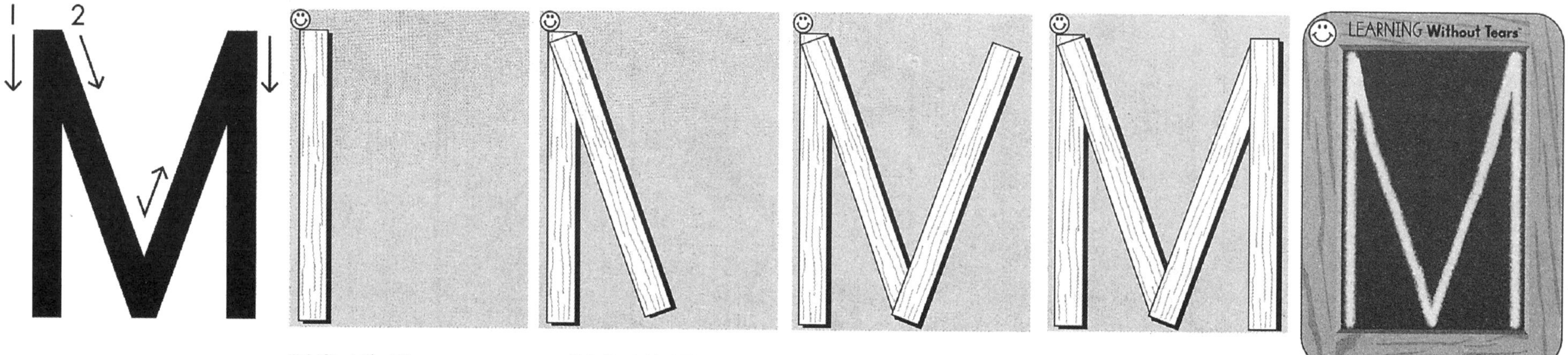

1 2

M

BIG LINE + BIG LINE + BIG LINE + BIG LINE

LEARNING Without Tears™

Trace M.

Copy M.

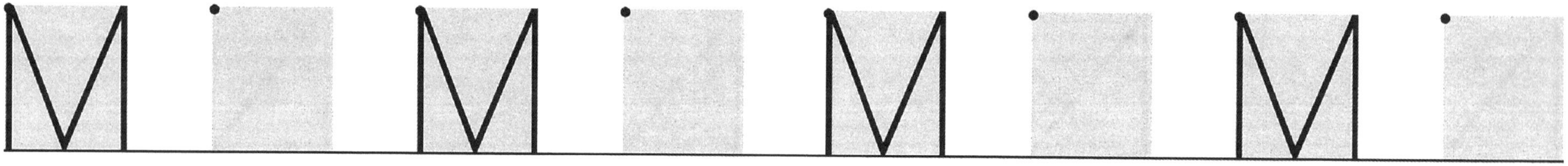

MONKEY

F 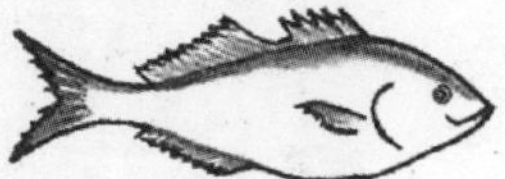

E 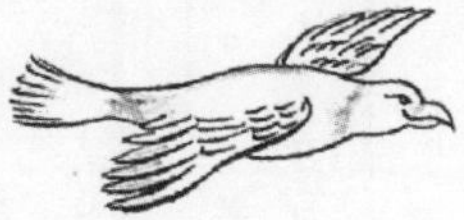

D 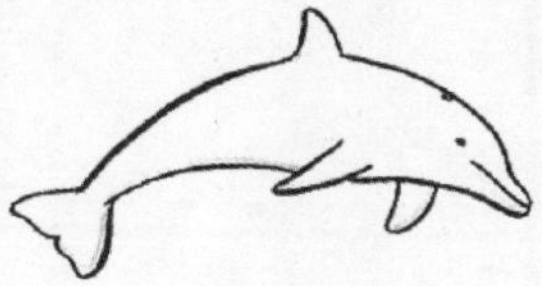

P 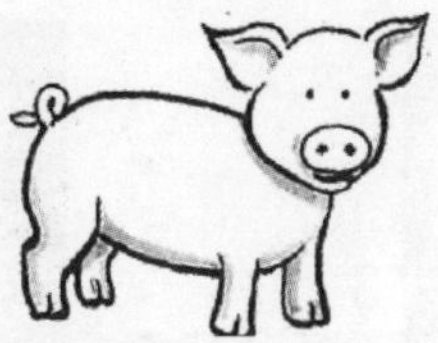

B 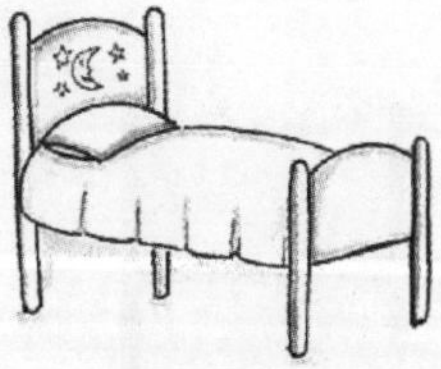

R 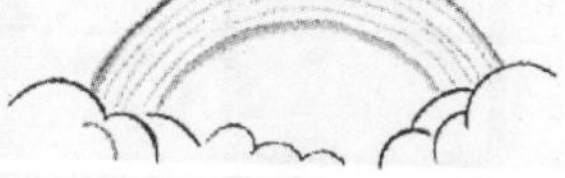

N 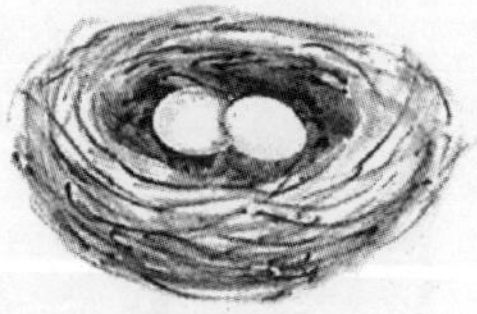

M 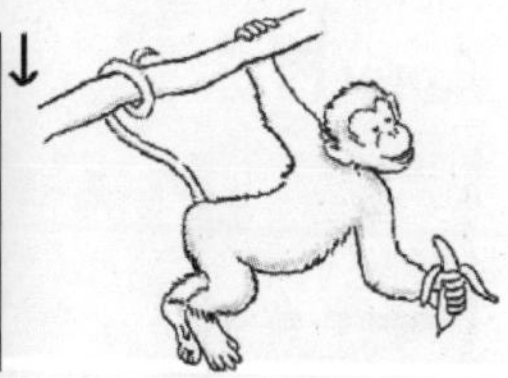

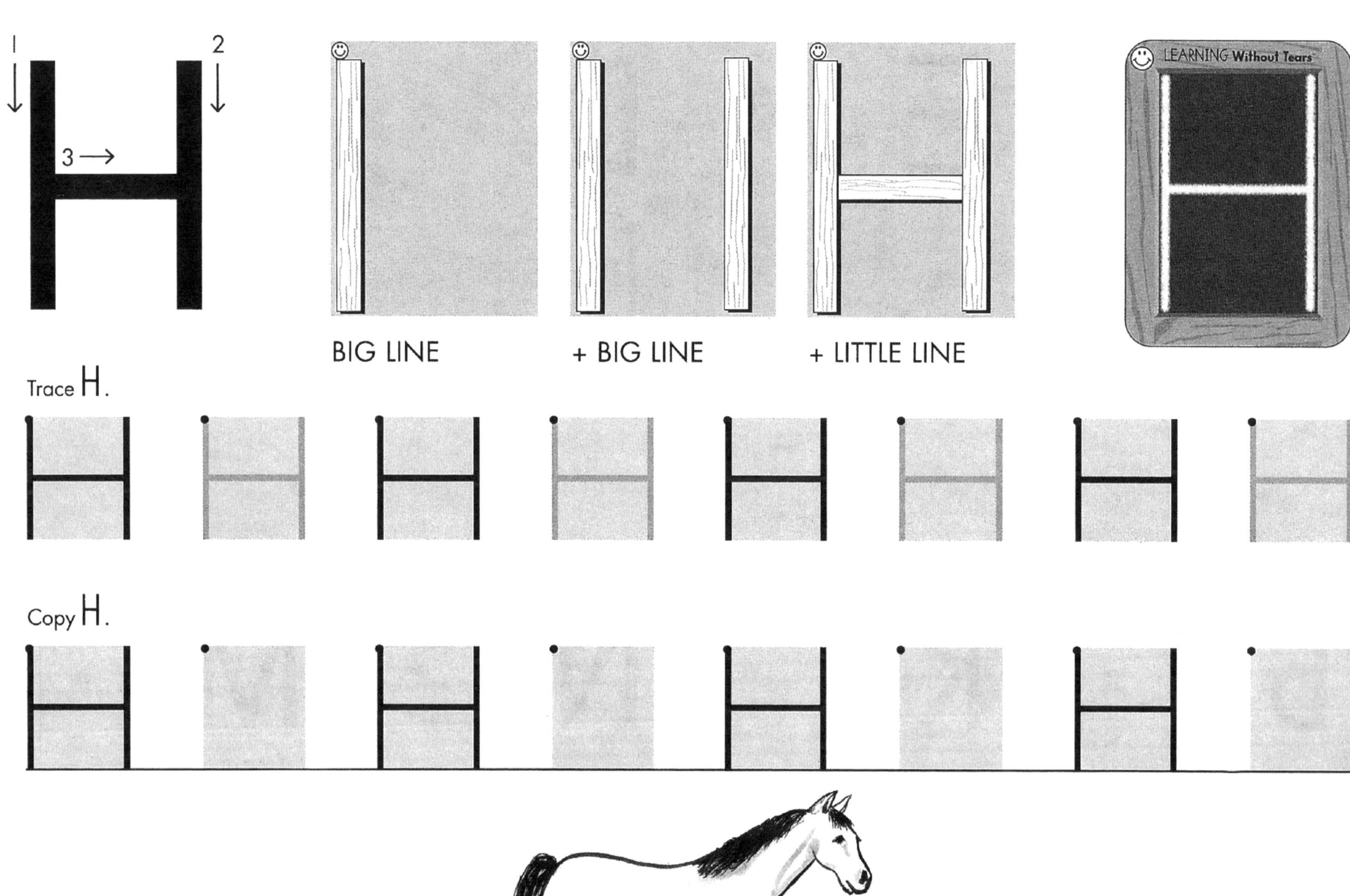

HORSE

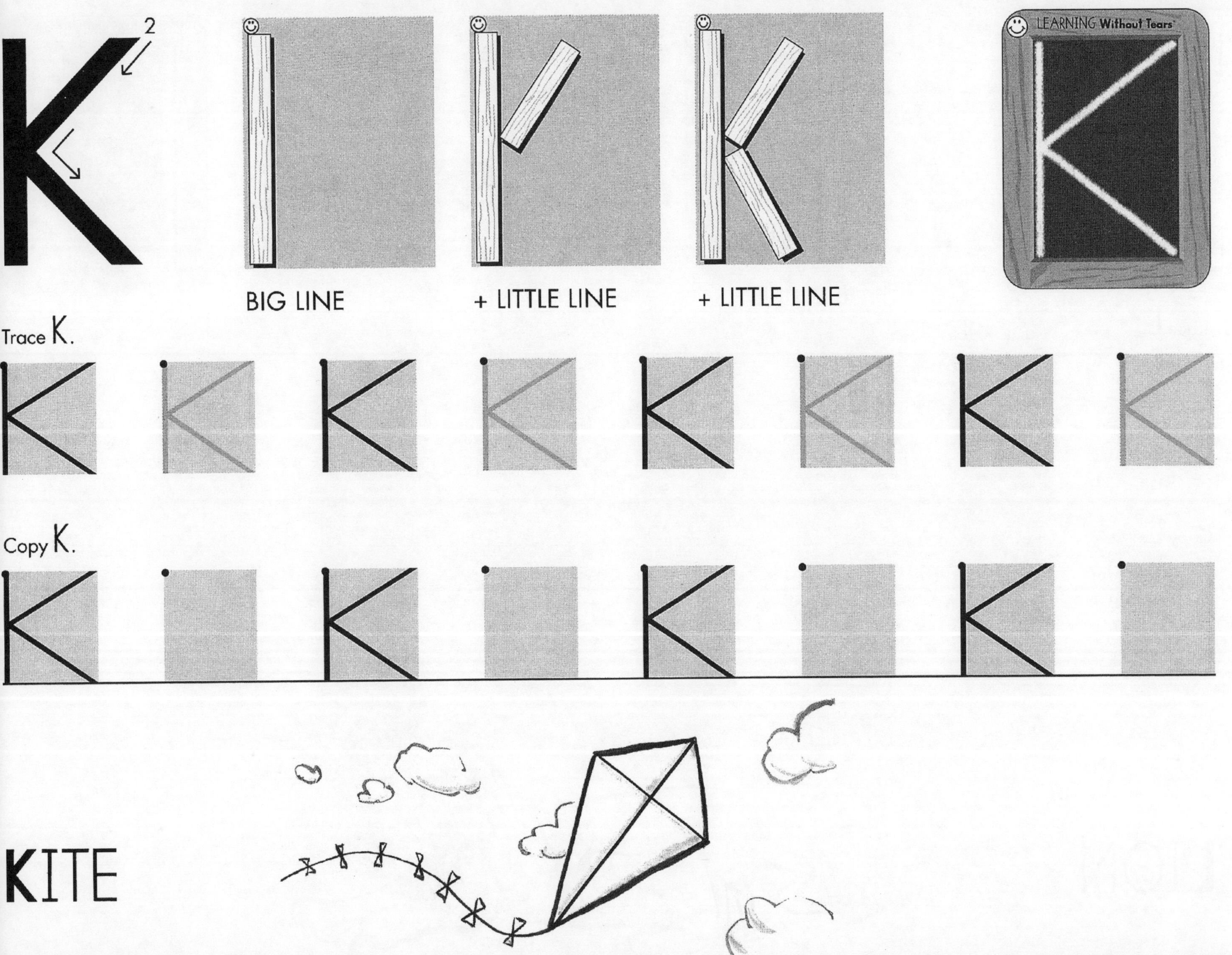

K
2
BIG LINE
+ LITTLE LINE
+ LITTLE LINE
LEARNING Without Tears
Trace K.
Copy K.
KITE

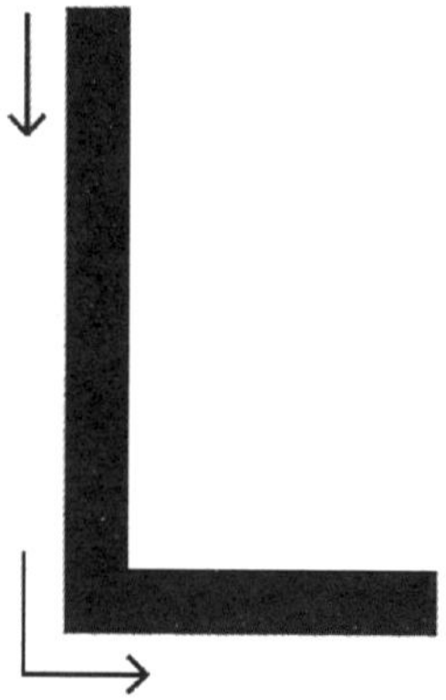

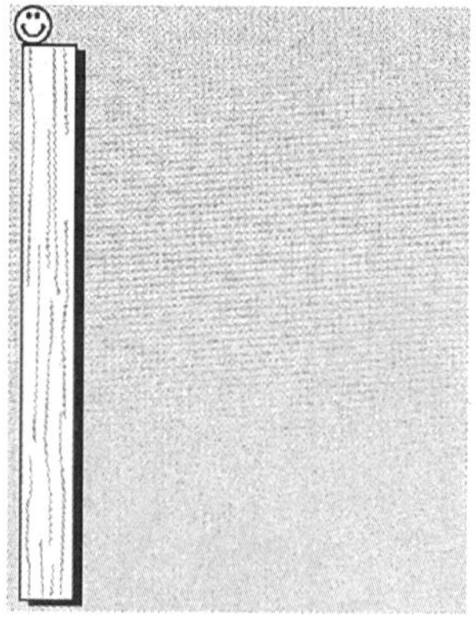

L

BIG LINE

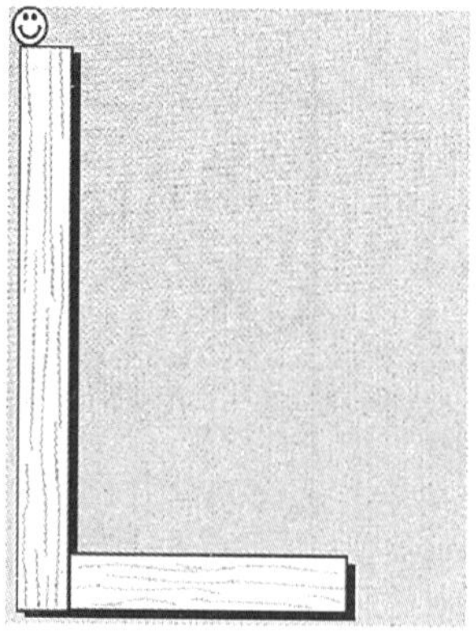

+ LITTLE LINE

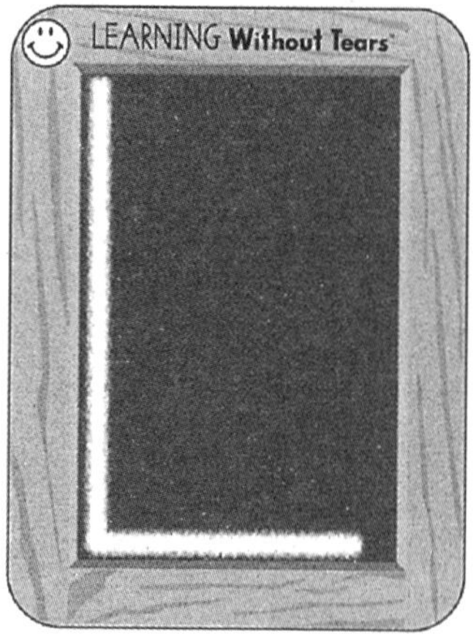

LEARNING Without Tears

Trace L.

Copy L.

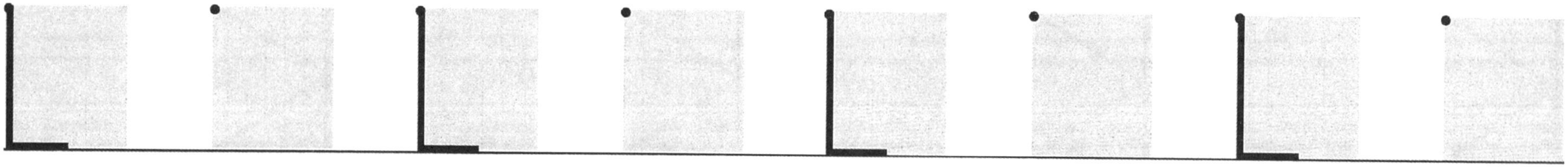

LION

Note: We do not use Wood Pieces to teach this letter.

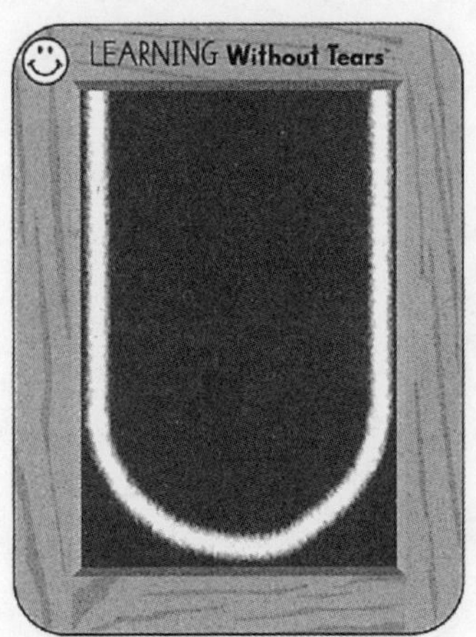

BIG LINE + TURN + BIG LINE

Trace U.

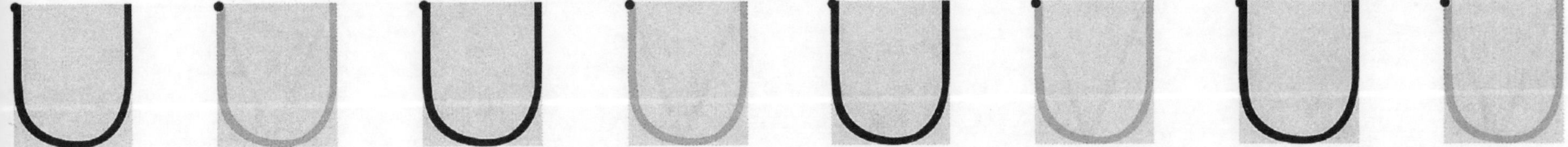

Copy U.

UNICORN

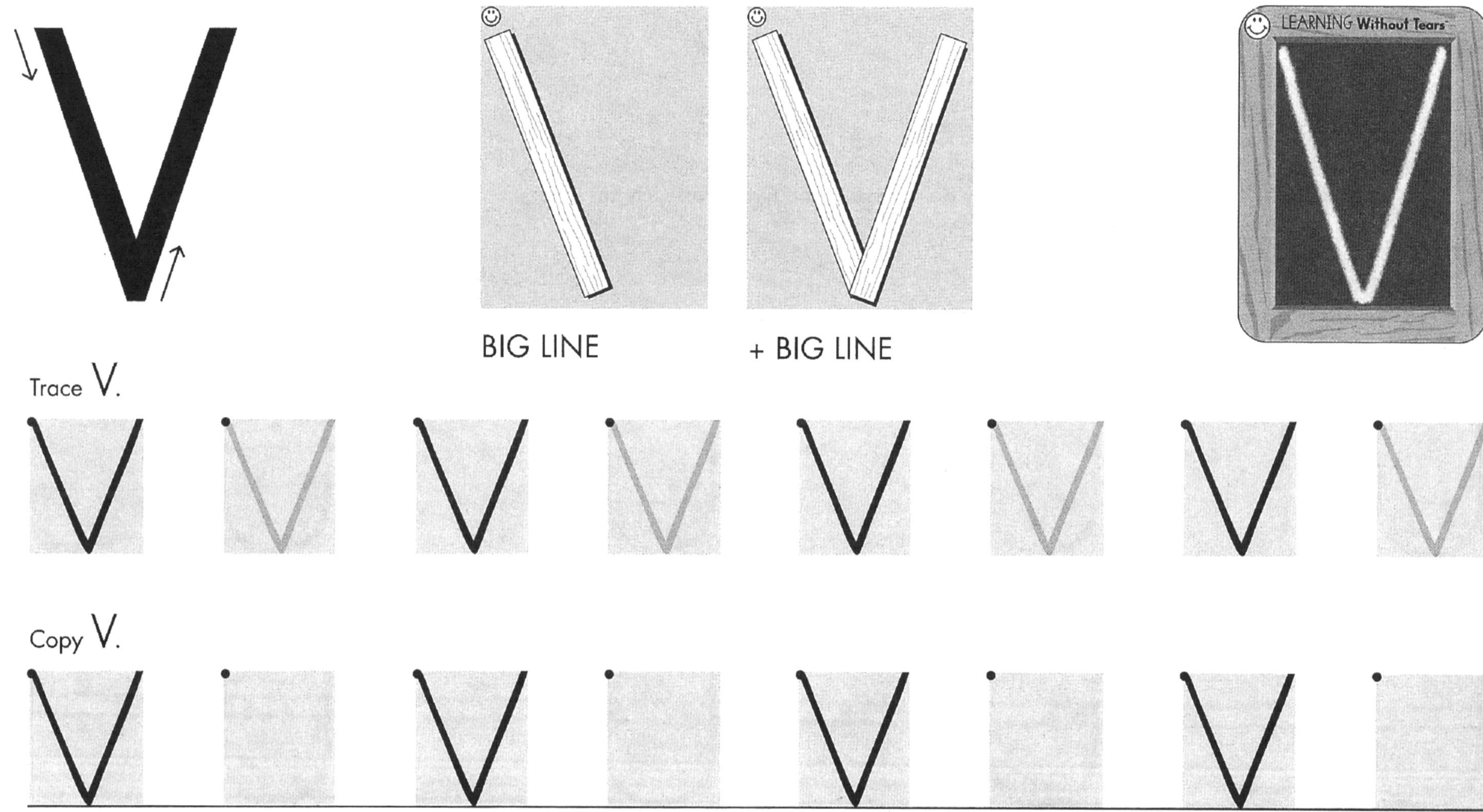

VOLCANO

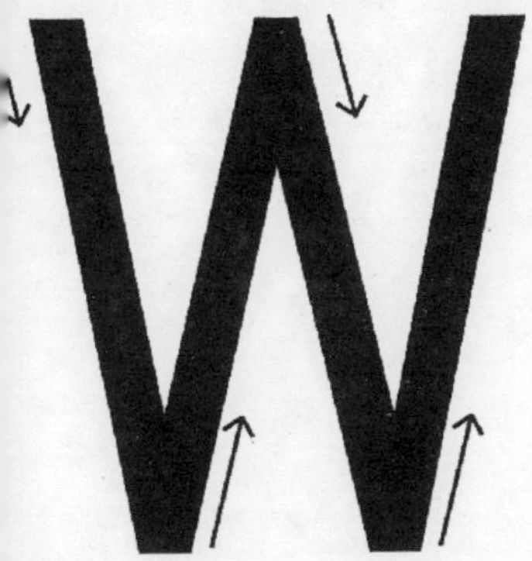

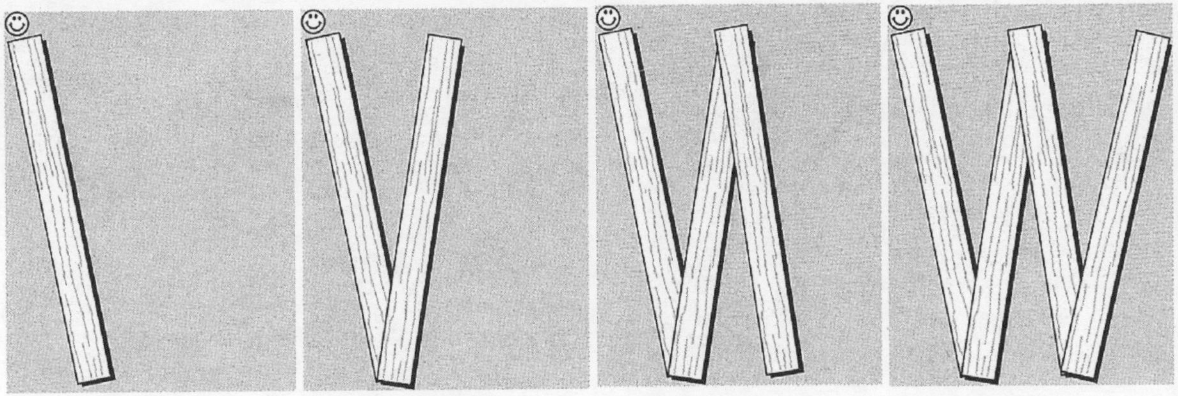

W

BIG LINE + BIG LINE + BIG LINE + BIG LINE

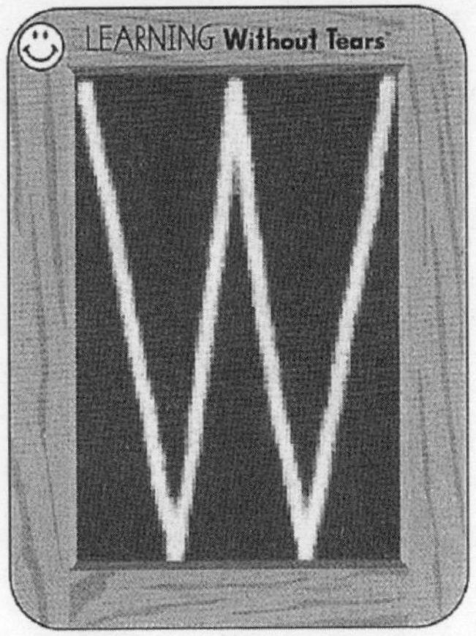

Trace W.

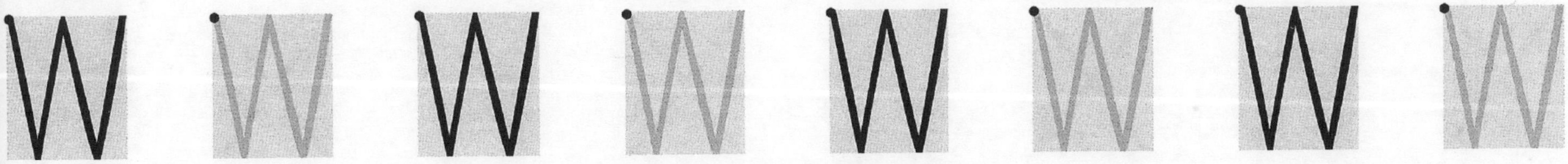

W W W W W W W W

Copy W.

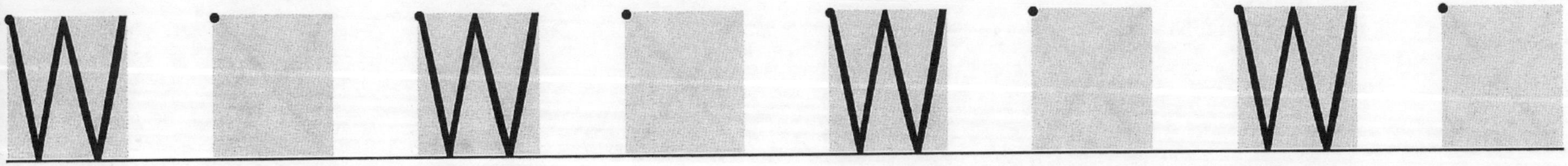

W W W W

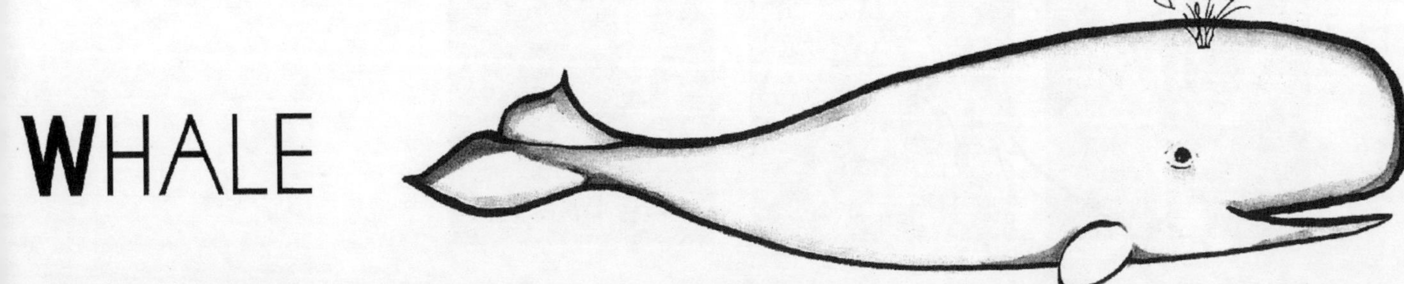

WHALE

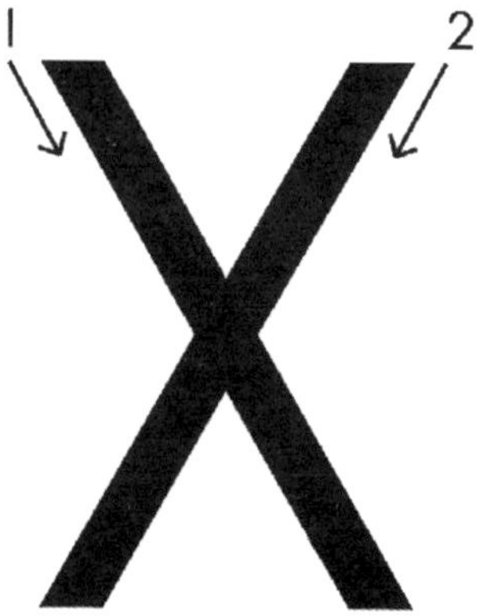

1 2

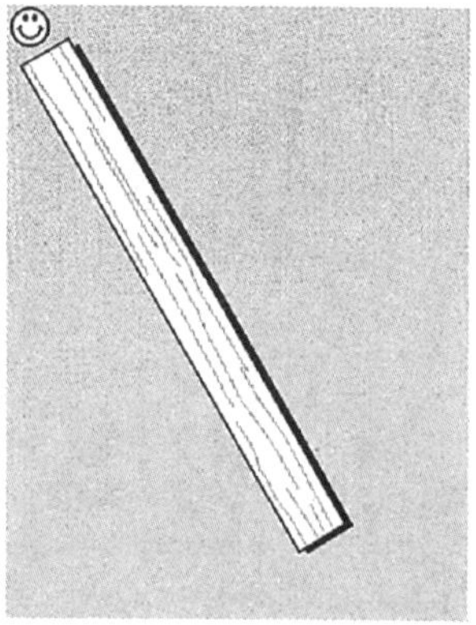

X

BIG LINE 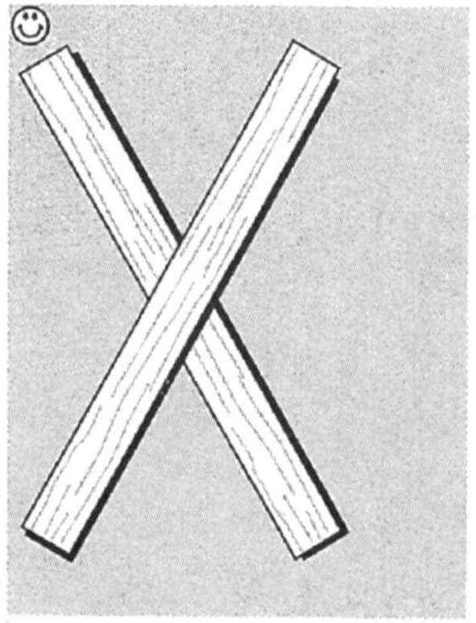 + BIG LINE

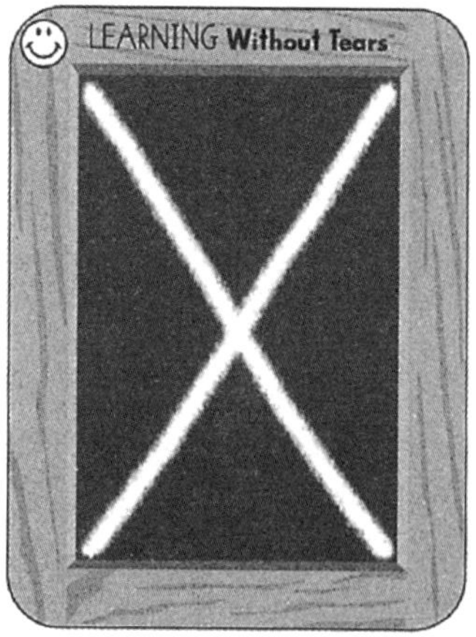

LEARNING Without Tears

Trace X.

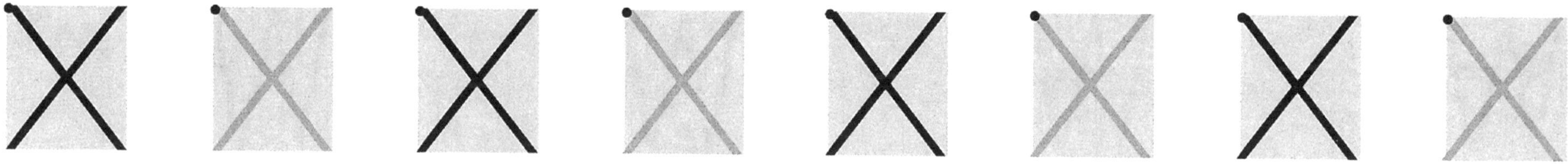

Copy X.

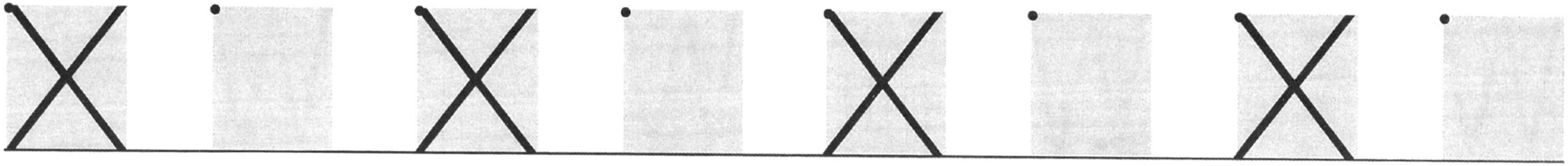

X-RAYS

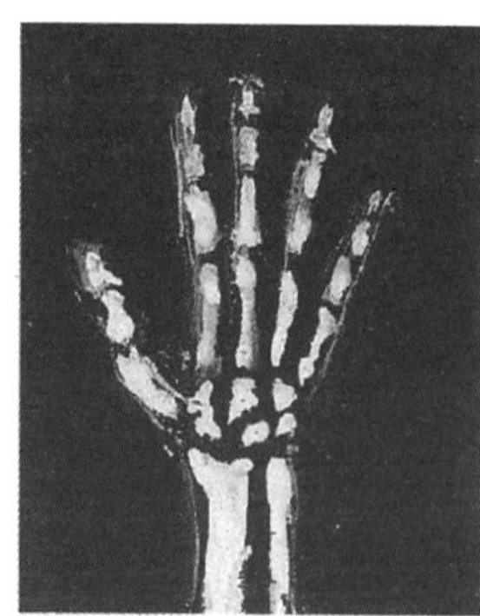

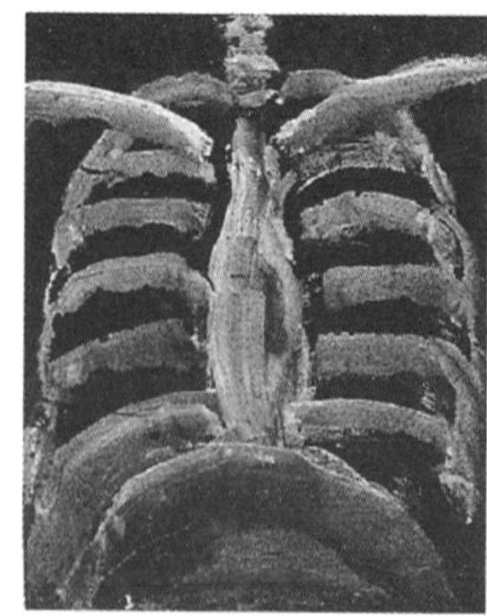

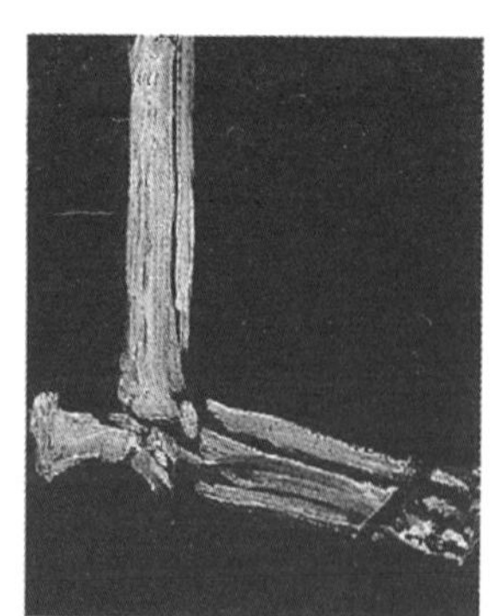

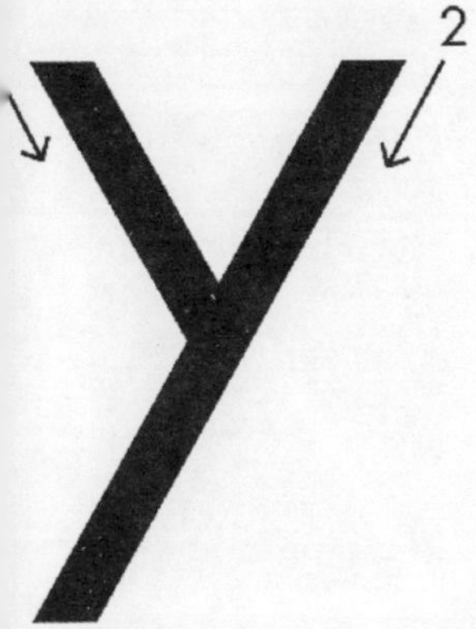

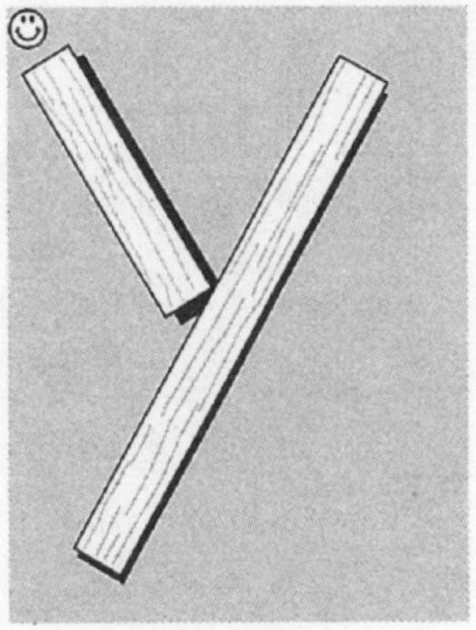

y

LITTLE LINE + BIG LINE

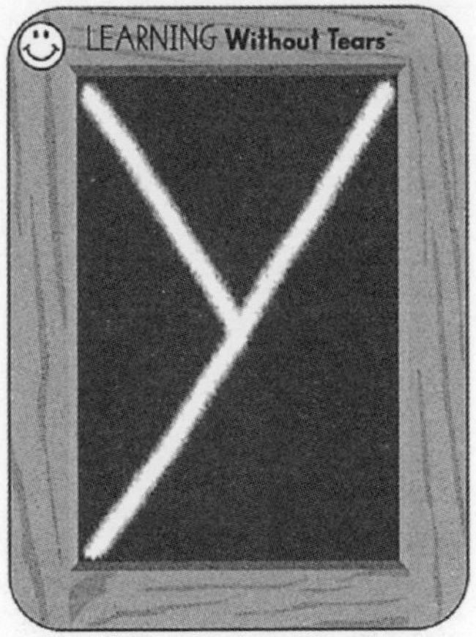

LEARNING Without Tears

Trace y.

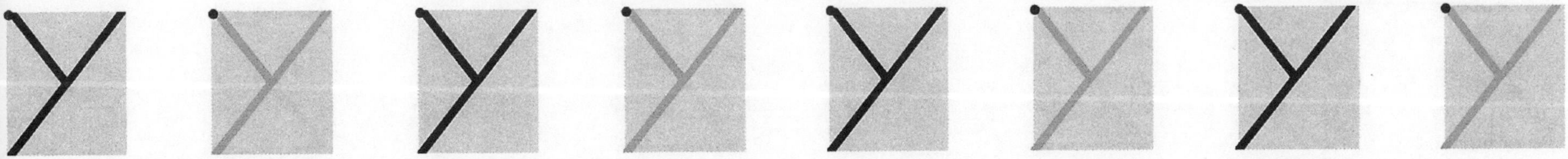

Copy y.

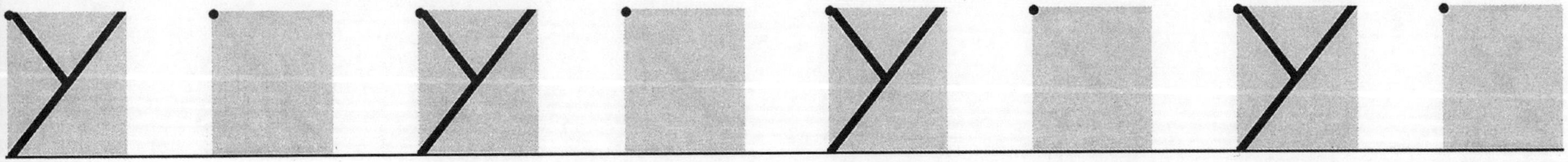

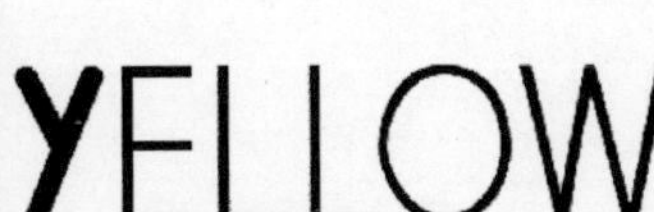

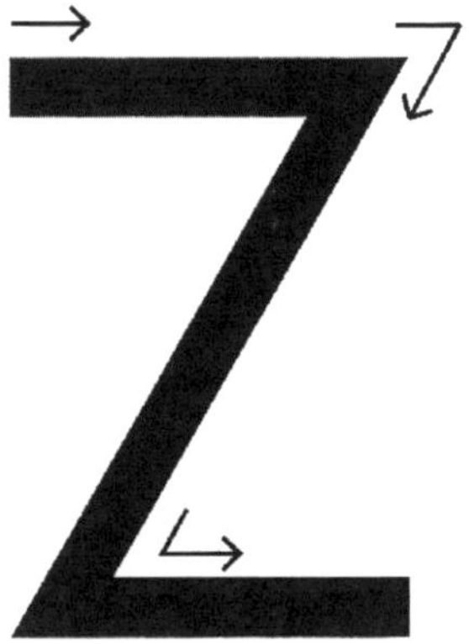

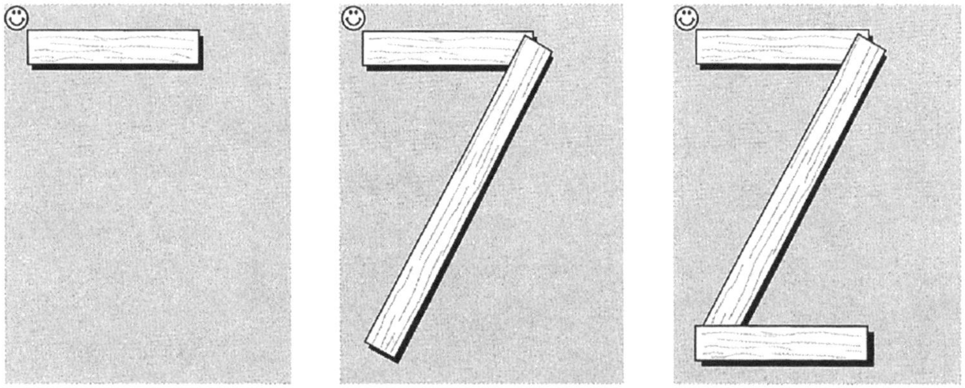

Z

LITTLE LINE

+ BIG LINE

+ LITTLE LINE

LEARNING Without Tears

Trace Z.

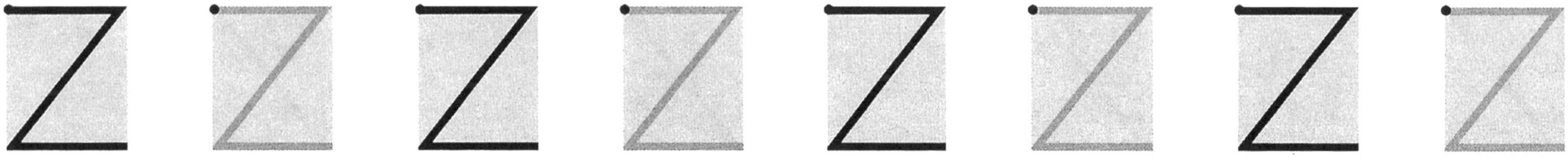

Z Z Z Z Z Z Z Z

Copy Z.

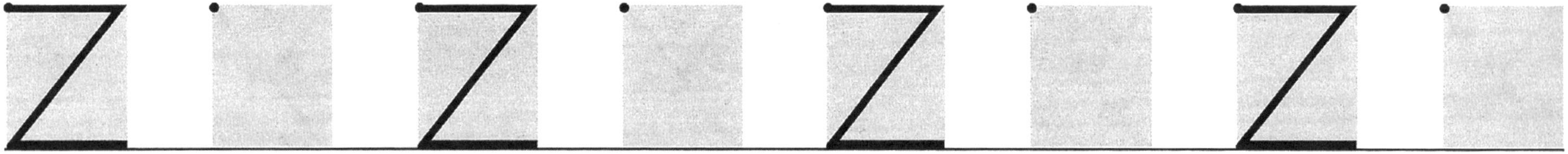

Z Z Z Z

ZEBRA

H

K

L

U

V

W

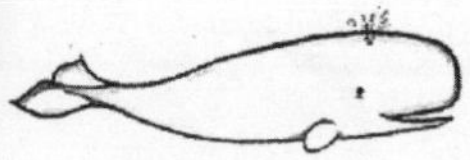

X

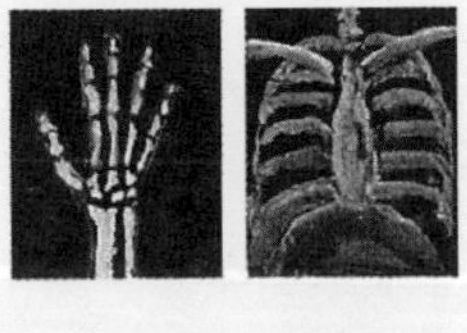

Y

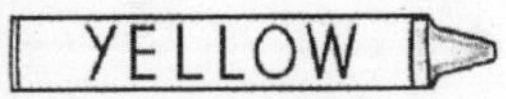

YELLOW

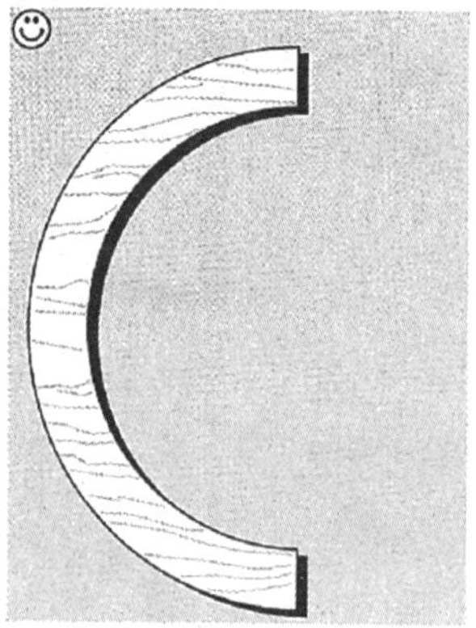

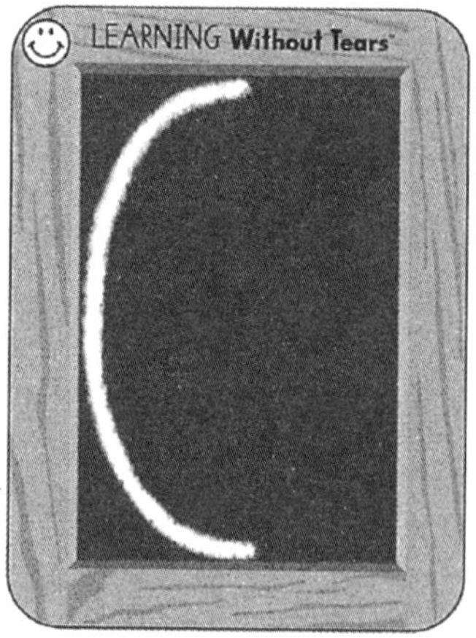

LEARNING Without Tears

BIG CURVE

Trace C.

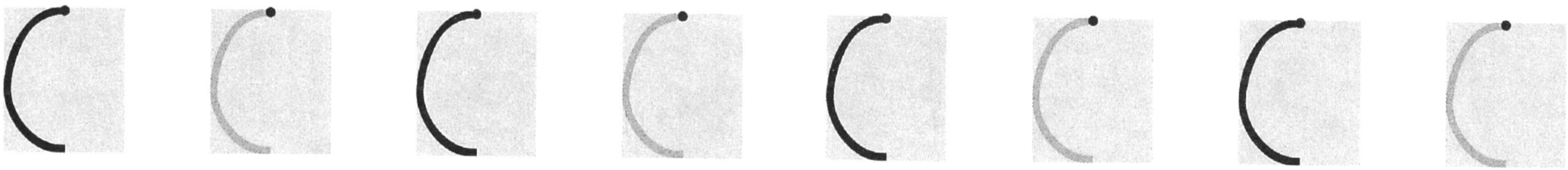

Copy C.

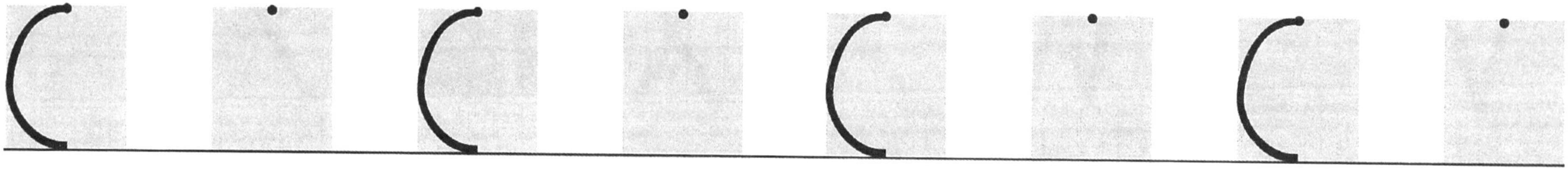

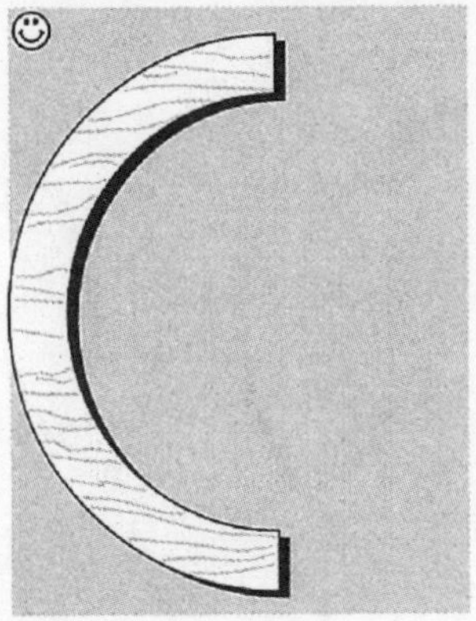

LEARNING Without Tears

BIG CURVE 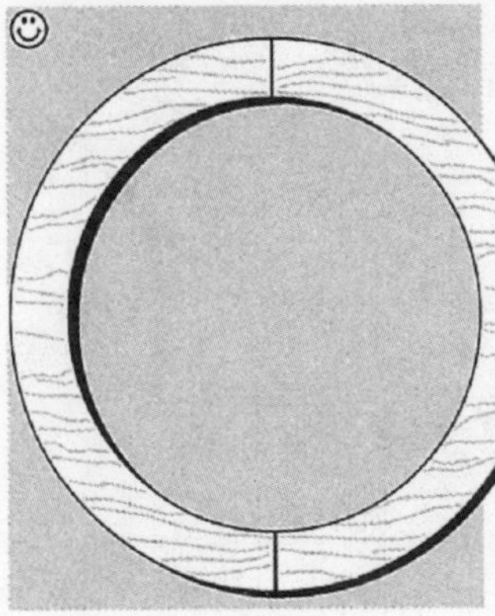 + BIG CURVE

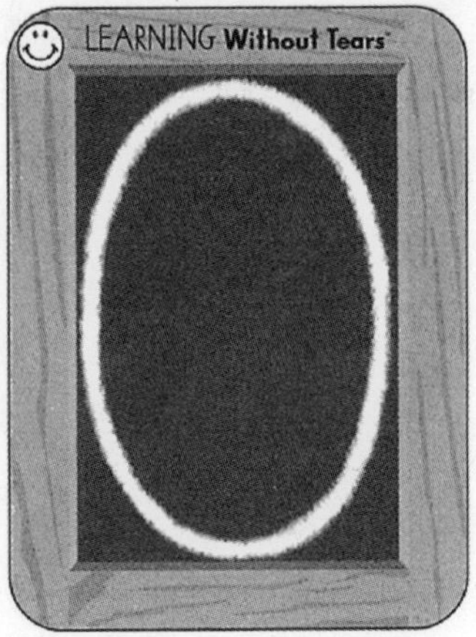

Trace O.

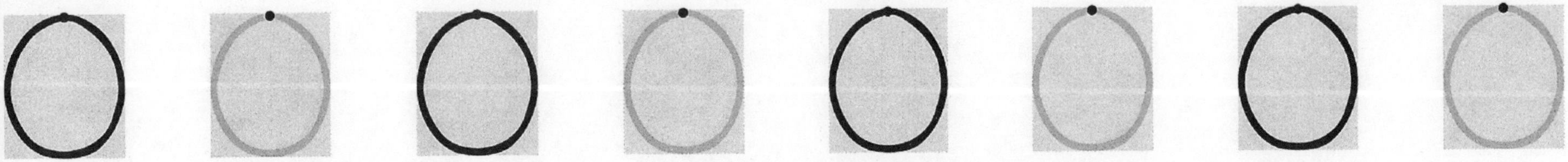

Copy O.

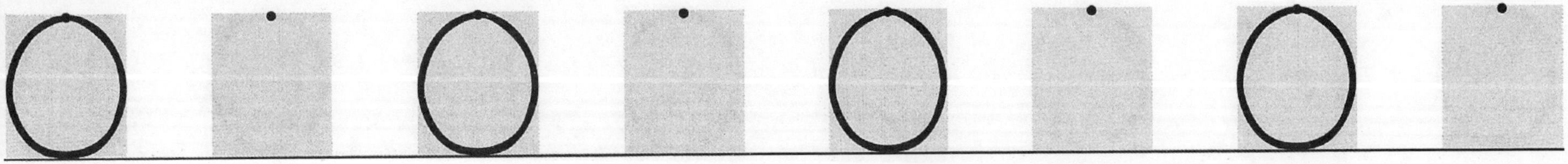

OCTOPUS

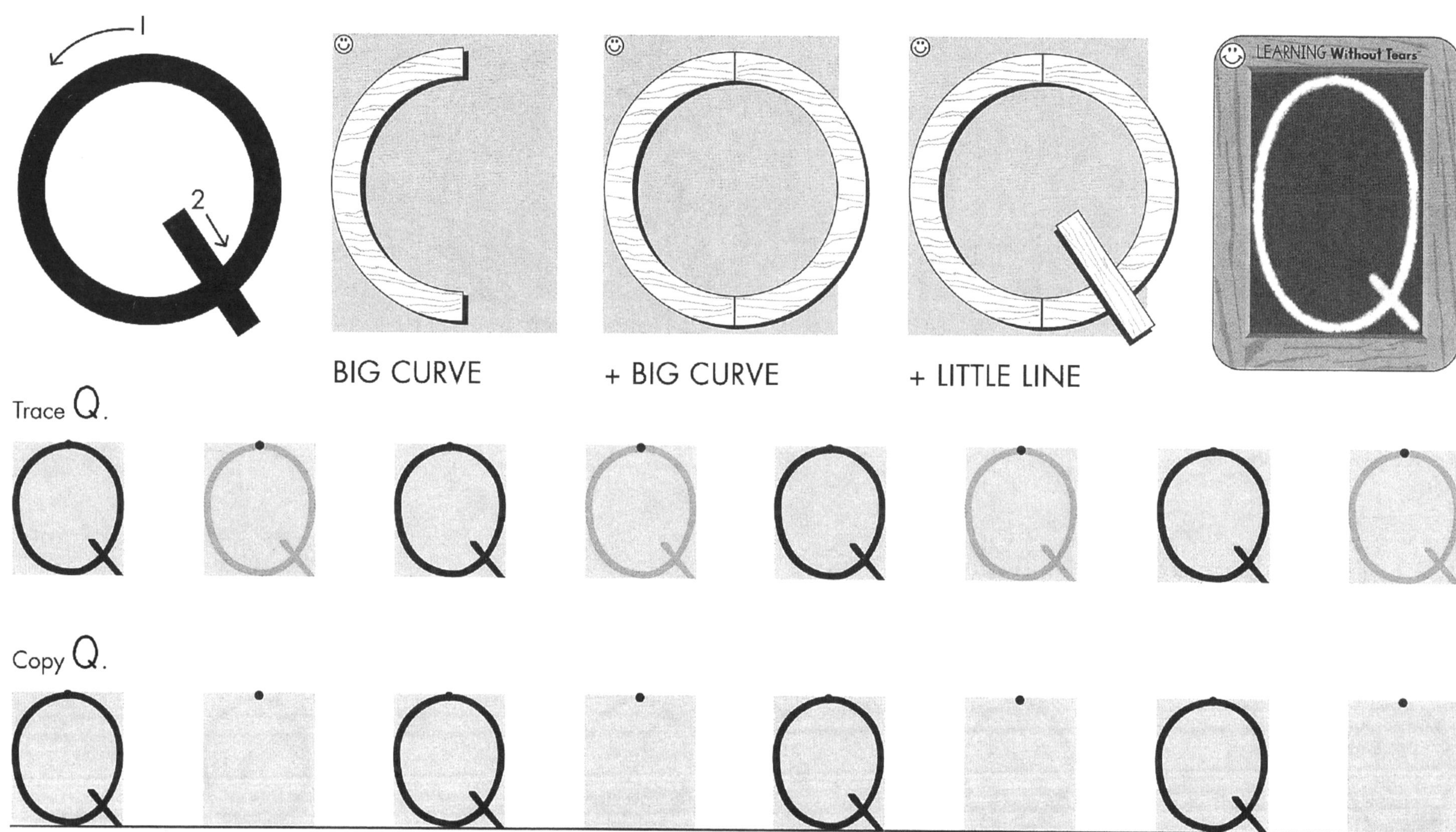

Trace Q.

Copy Q.

QUEEN

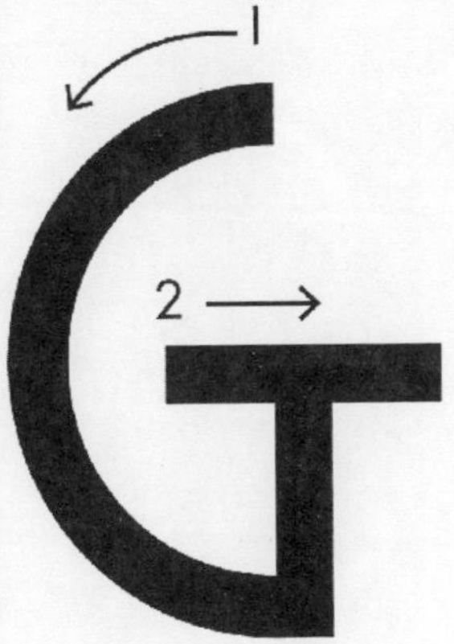

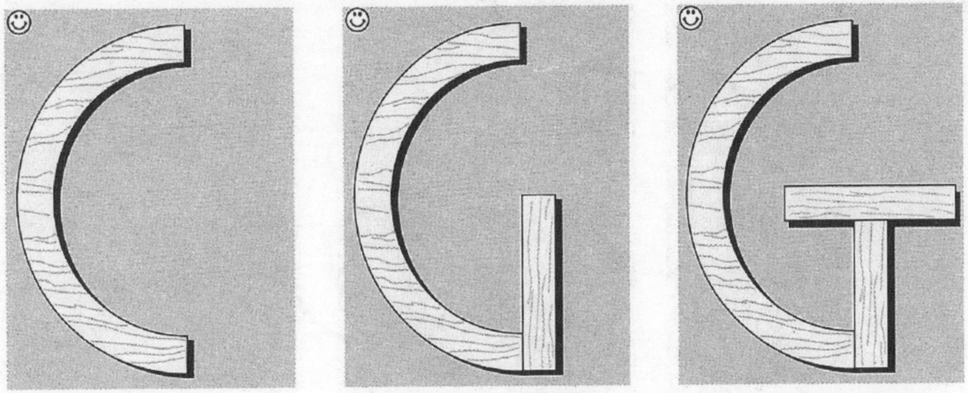

G

BIG CURVE + LITTLE LINE + LITTLE LINE

LEARNING Without Tears

Trace G.

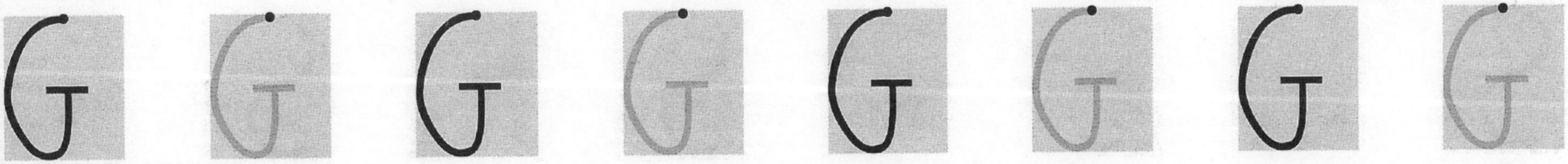

Copy G.

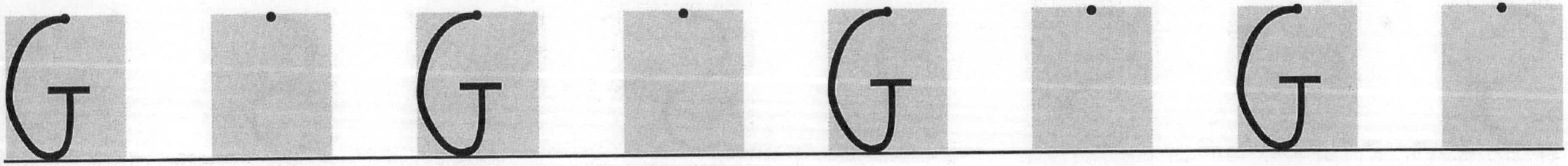

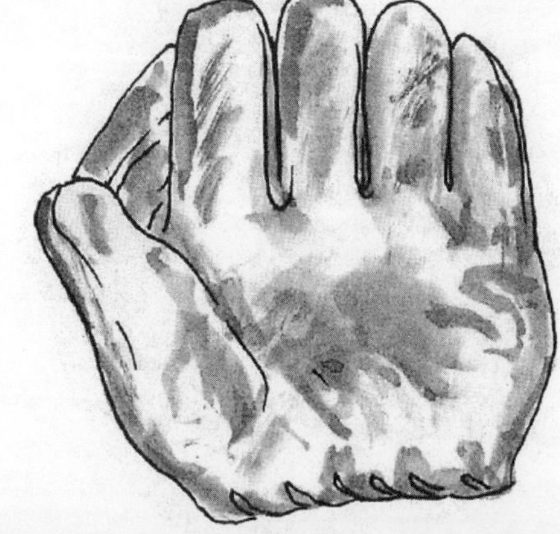

GLOVE

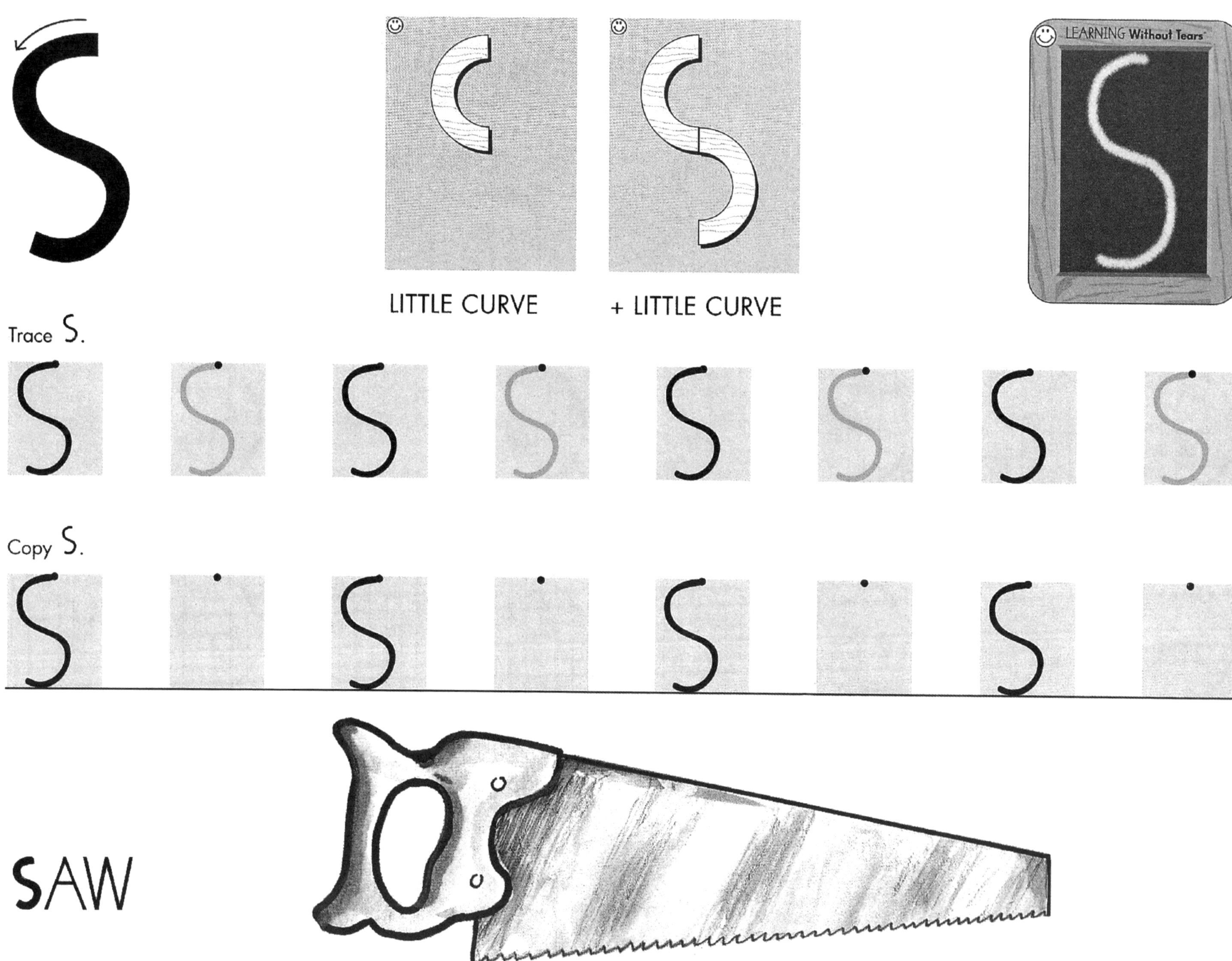
LEARNING Without Tears
LITTLE CURVE
+ LITTLE CURVE
Trace S.
Copy S.
SAW

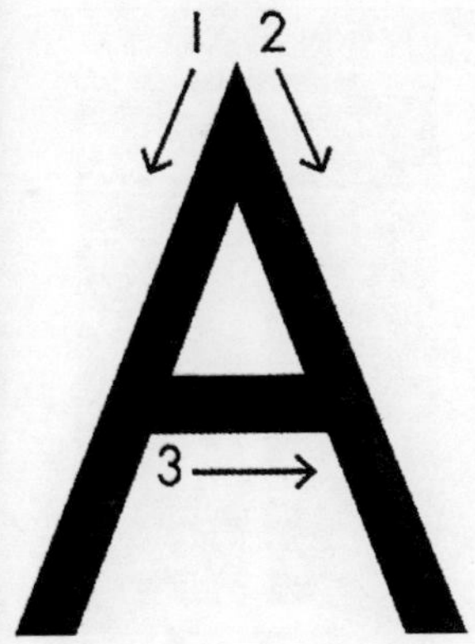

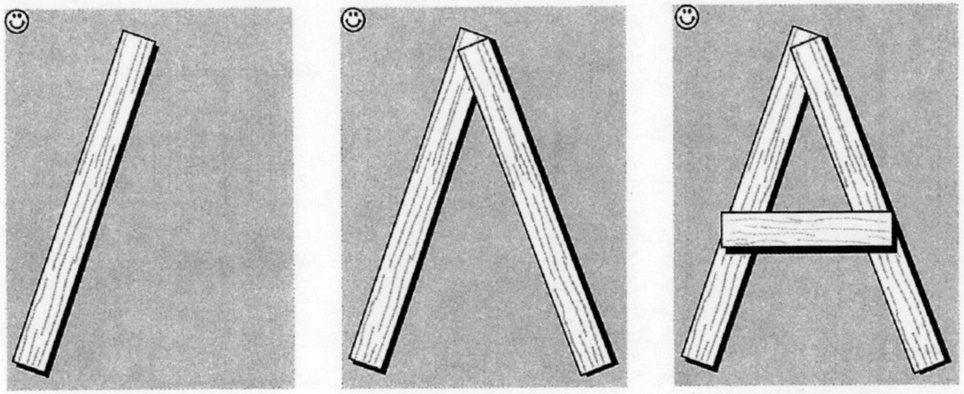

1 2

A

3

BIG LINE + BIG LINE + LITTLE LINE

LEARNING Without Tears

Trace A.

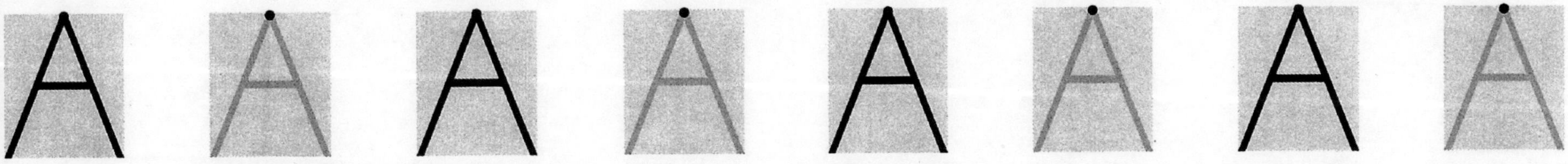

A A A A A A A A

Copy A.

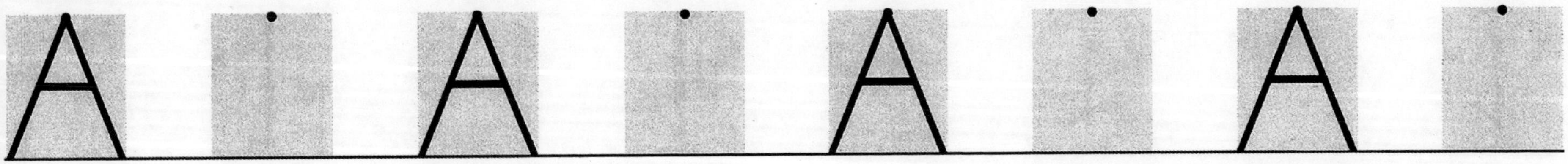

A A A A

ANT

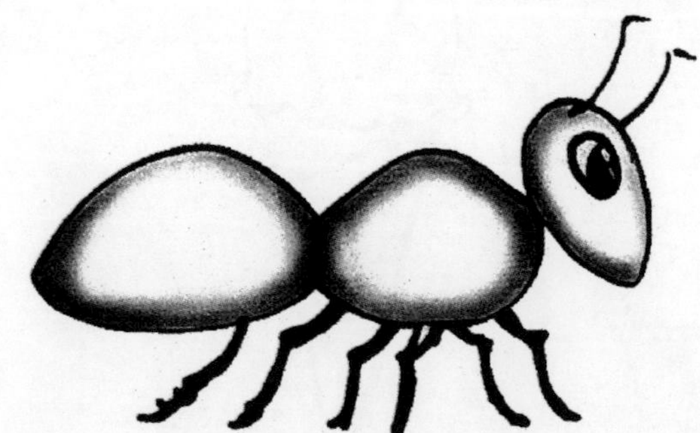

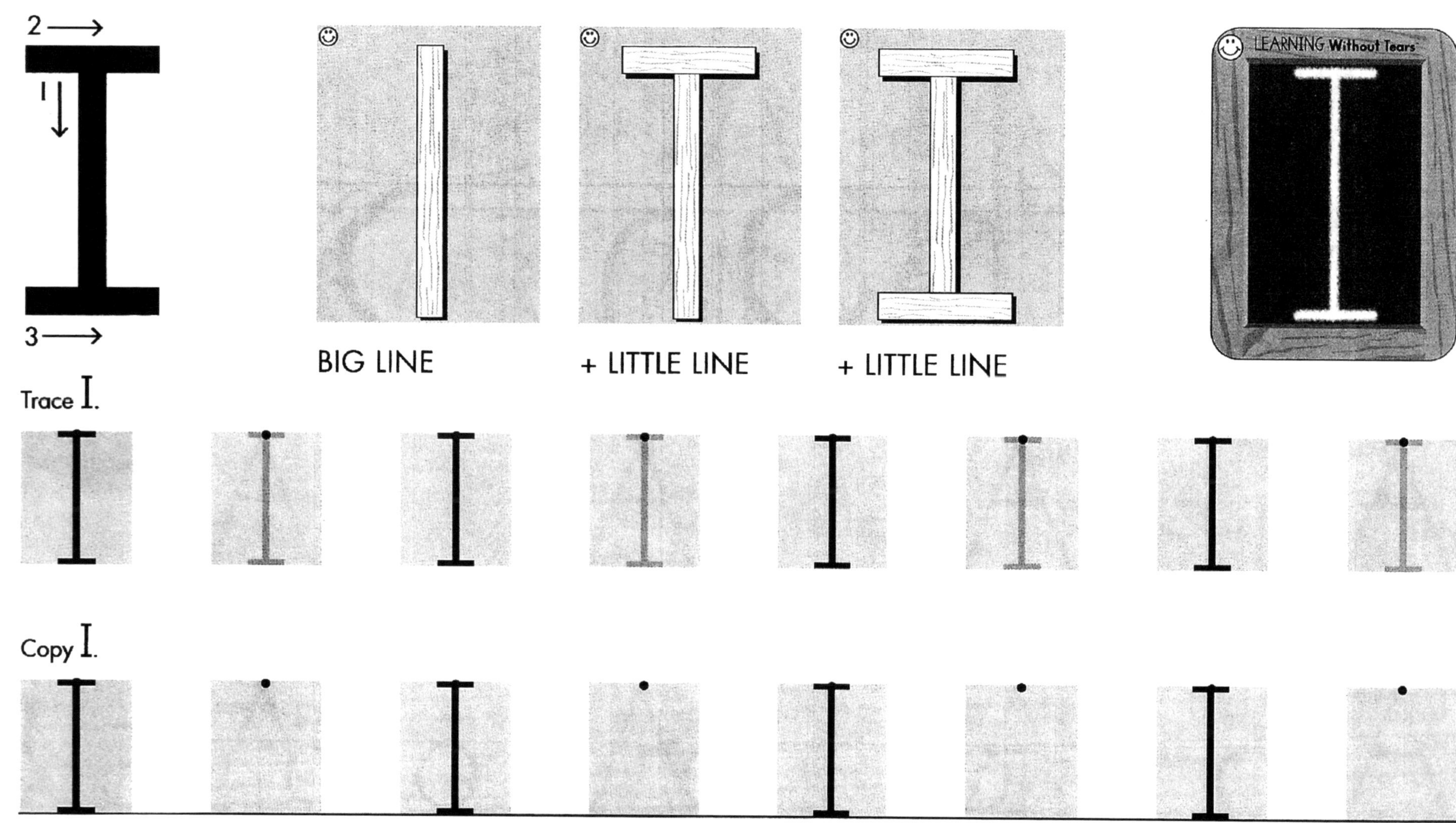

ICE CREAM

2
1
BIG LINE
+ LITTLE LINE
LEARNING Without Tears
Trace T.
Copy T.
TREES

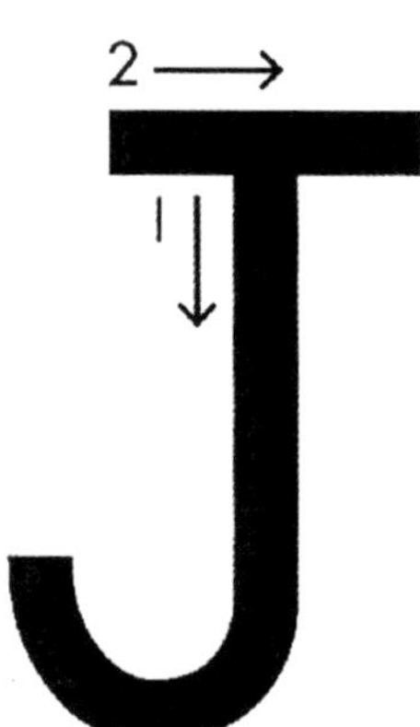

Note: We do not use Wood Pieces to teach this letter.

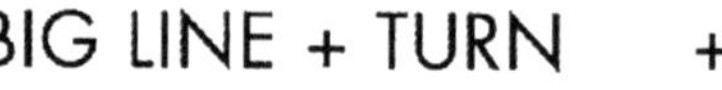

+ LITTLE LINE

Trace J.

   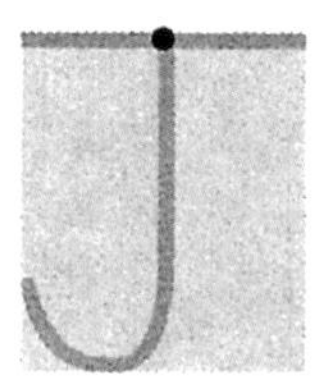  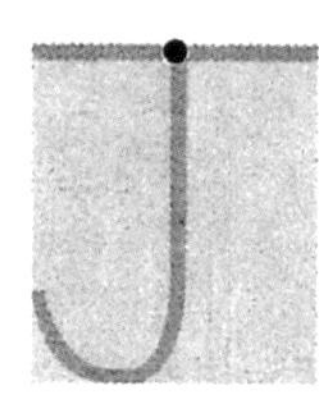  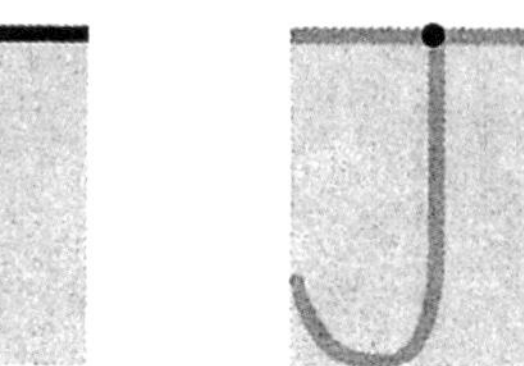

Copy J.

   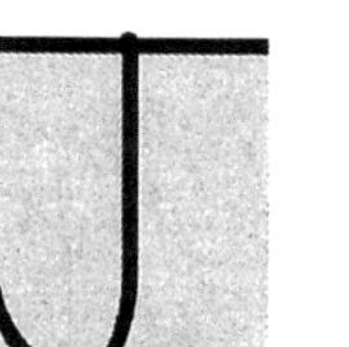  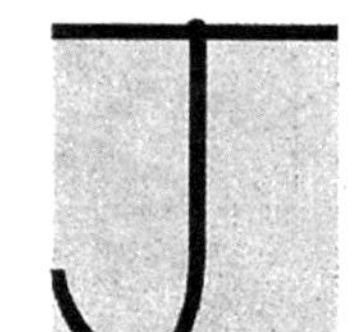 

C

O

Q

G

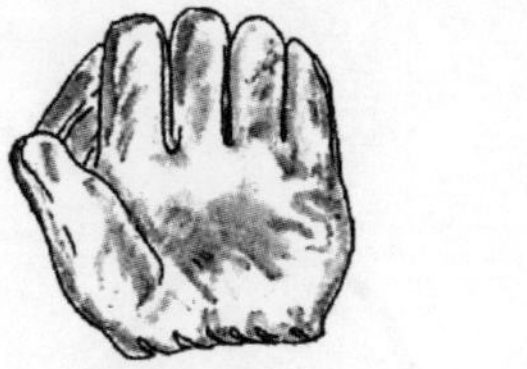

S

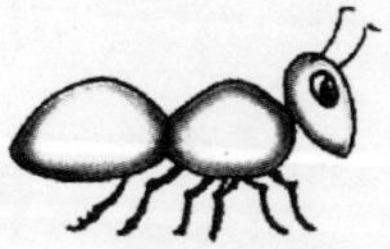

A

I

T

CAPITALS FOR ME

Start on the dot. Trace the capitals.

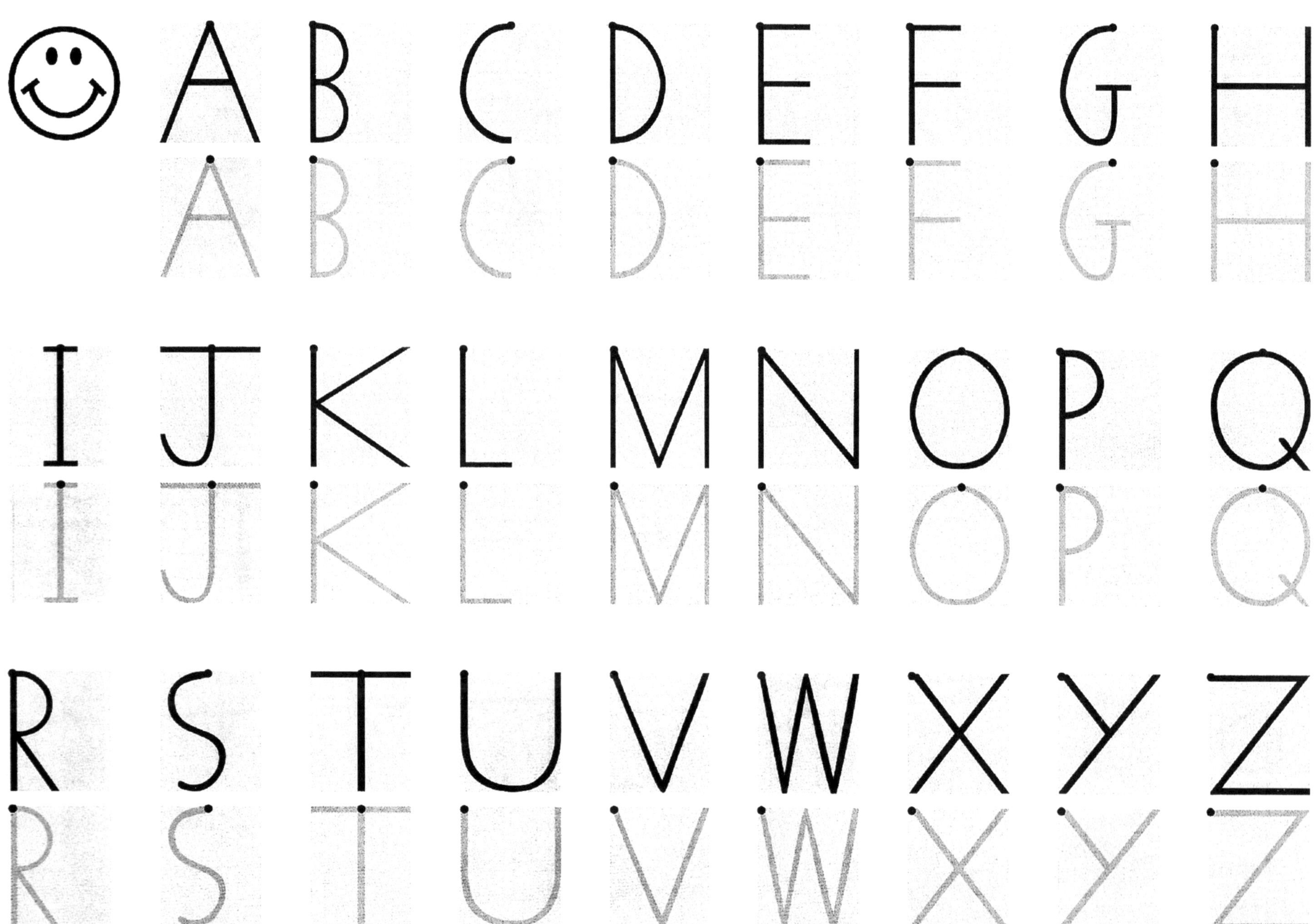

Lowercase Letters

Some are small.
Some are tall.
Some go below the line.

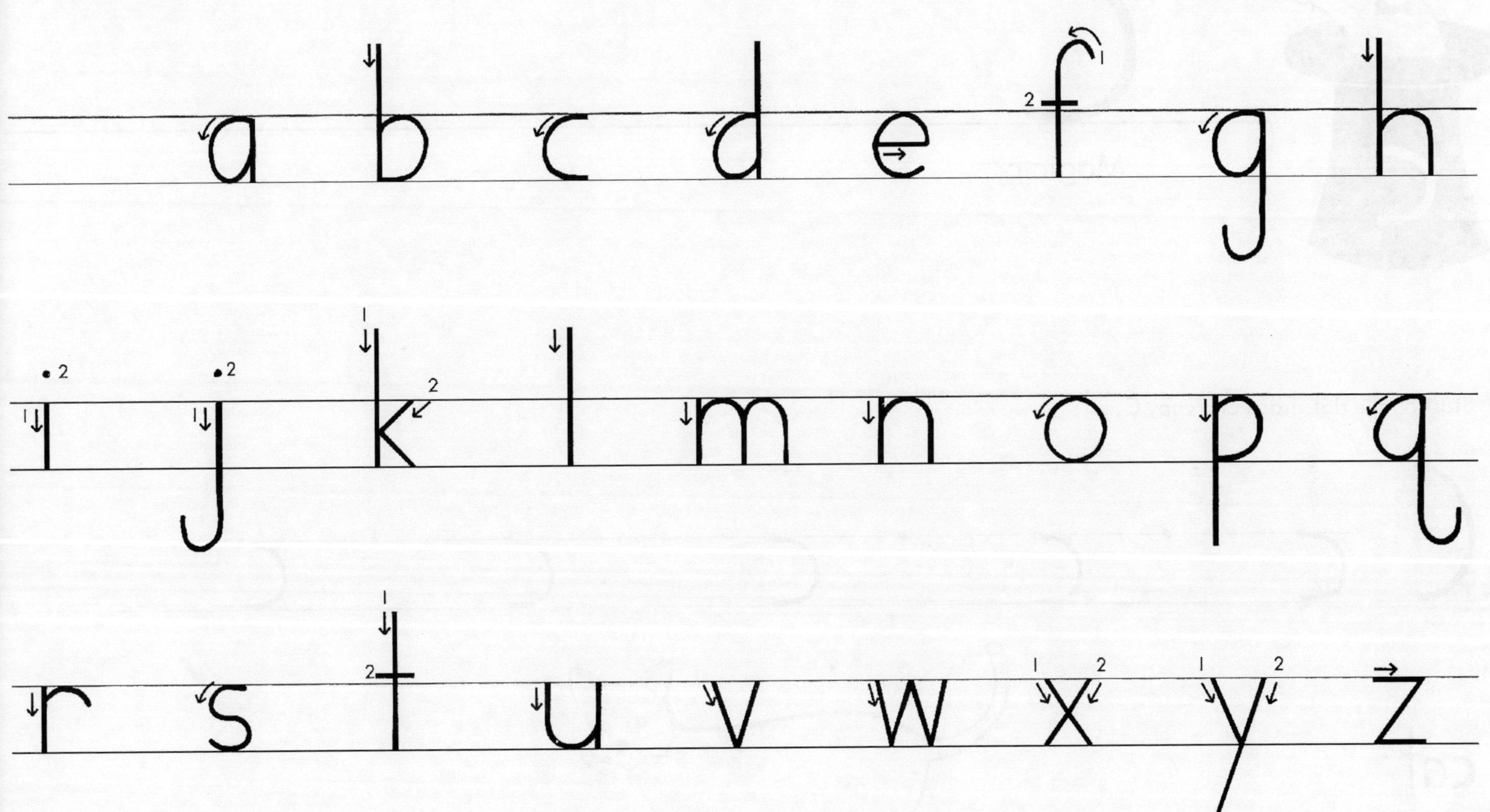

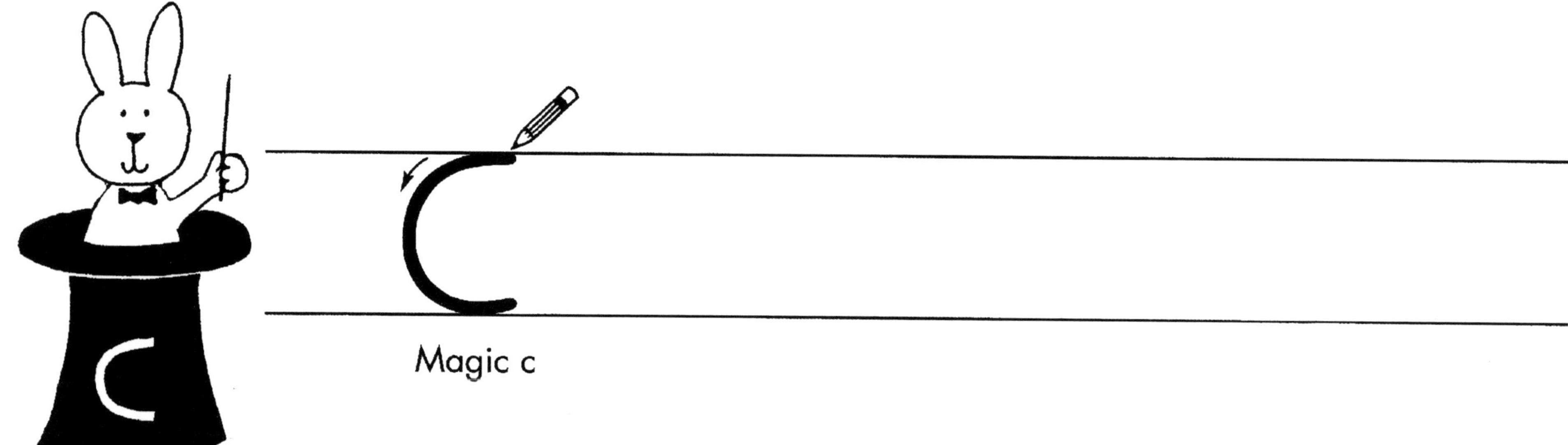

Start on the dot. Trace and copy c.

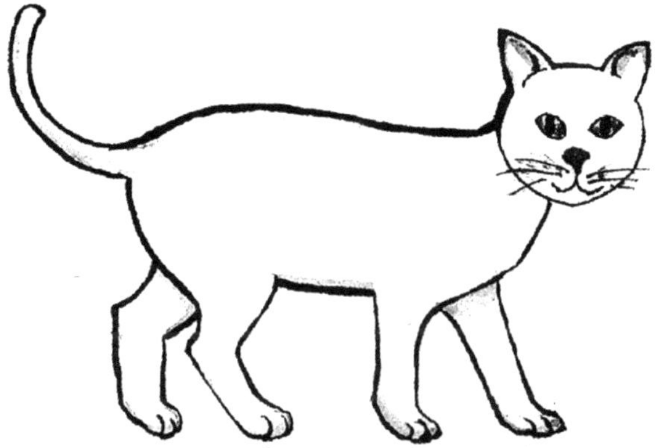

cat

Trace c.

Cc

cow

cat

city

cloud

Magic c keep going stop

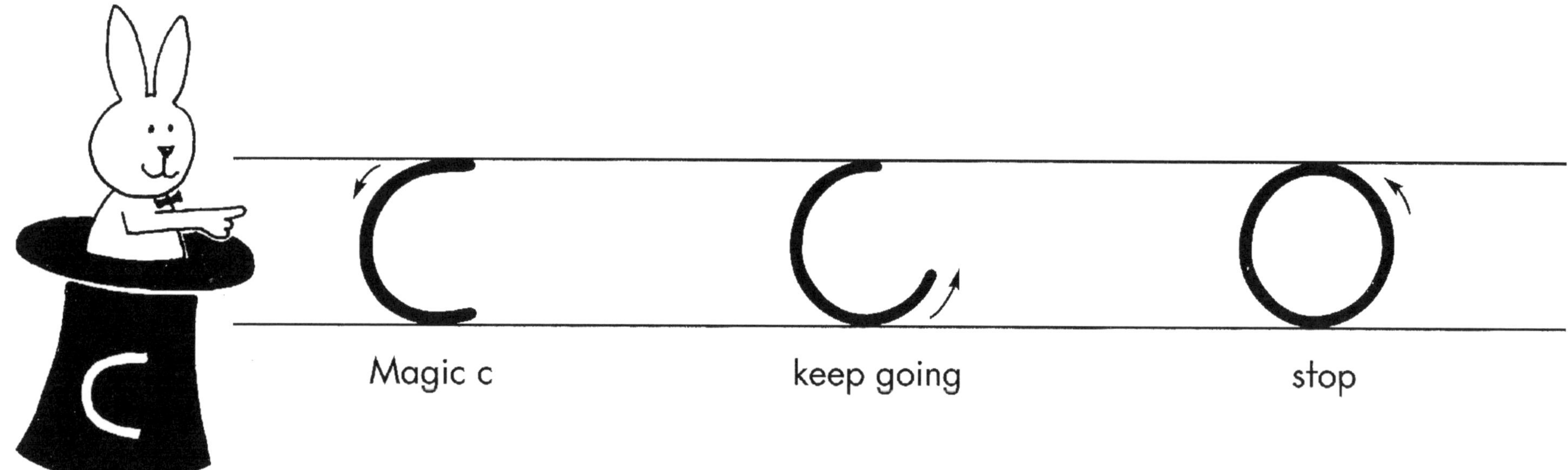

Start on the dot. Trace and copy o.

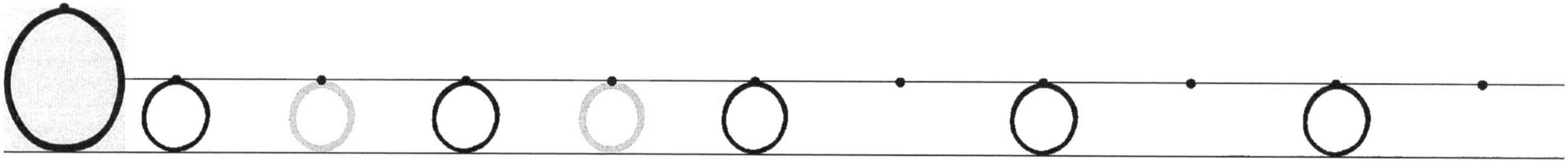

owl

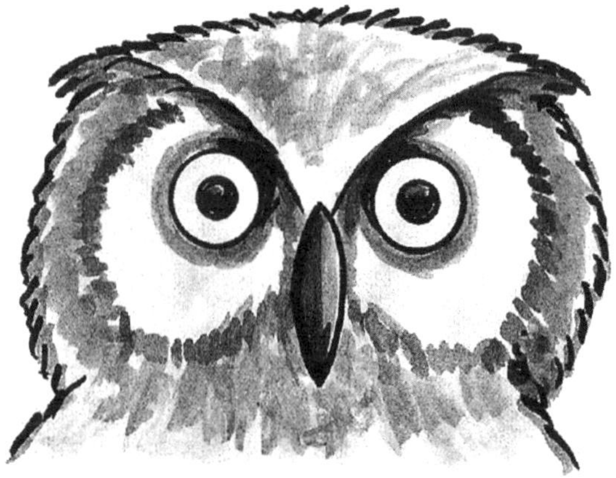

Trace o.

Oo

little
Magic c

little Magic c

turn down

curve around

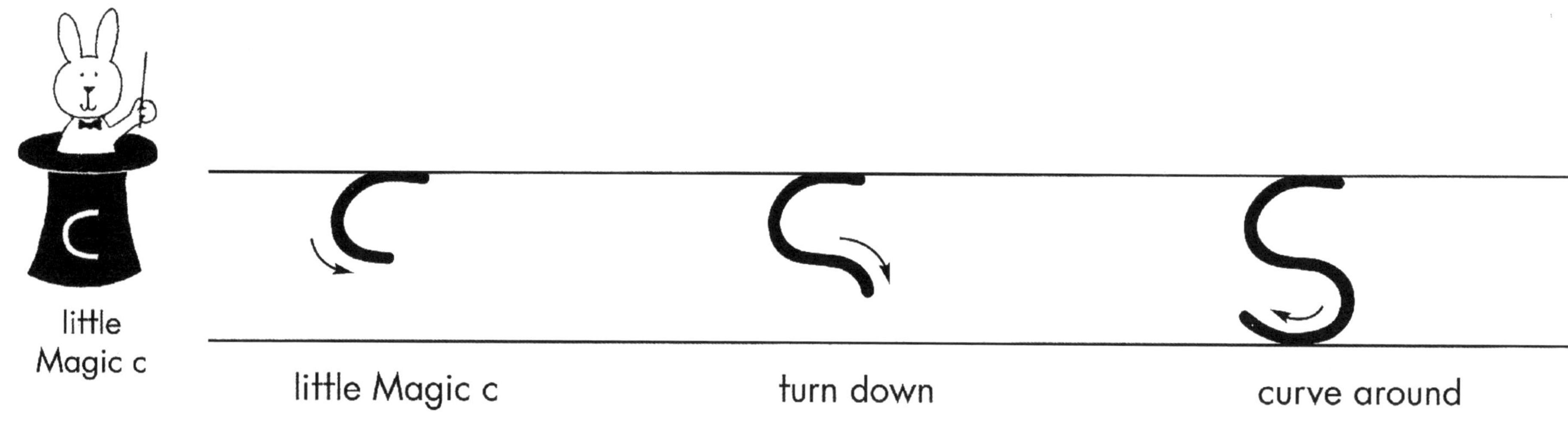

Start on the dot. Trace and copy **s**.

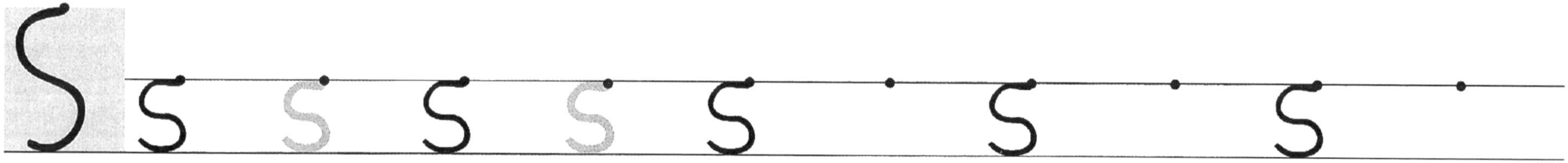

seal

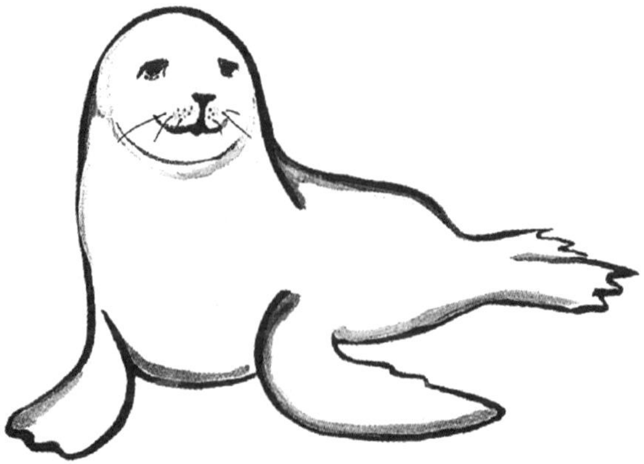

Start on the dot. Trace S s.

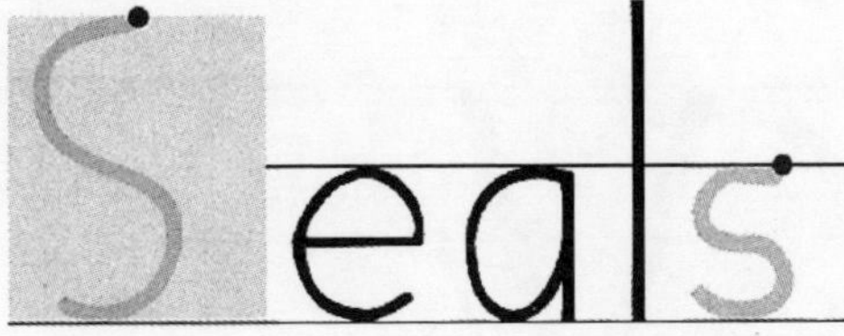

Seals swim.

Start on the dot. Trace C c.

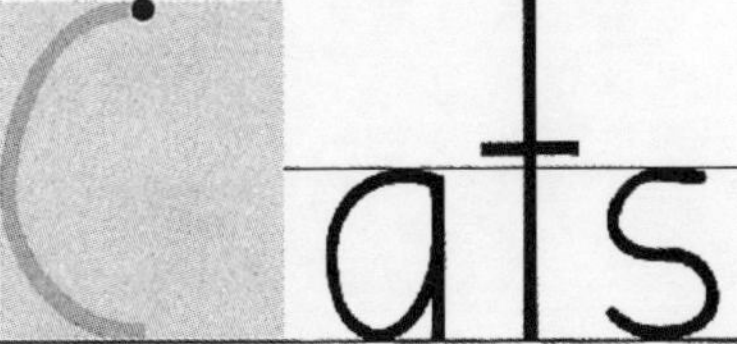

Cats climb.

Start on the dot. Trace O o.

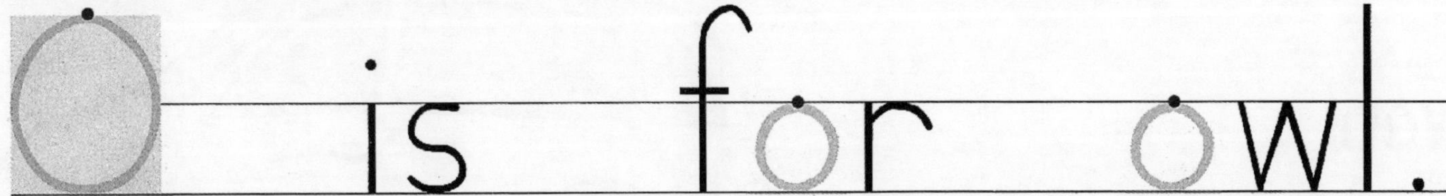

O is for owl.

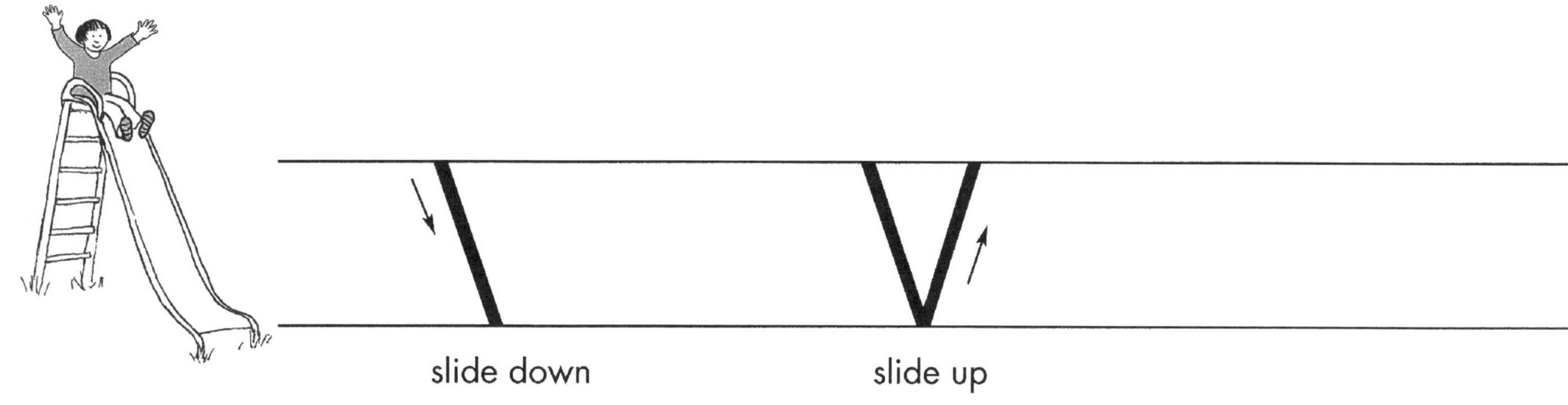

Start on the dot. Trace and copy **V**.

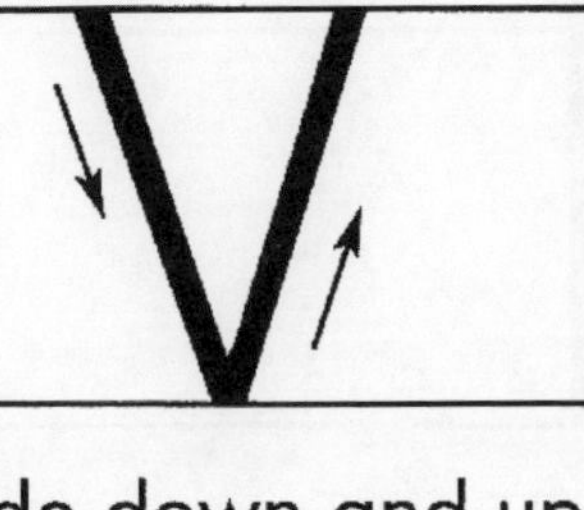

slide down and up

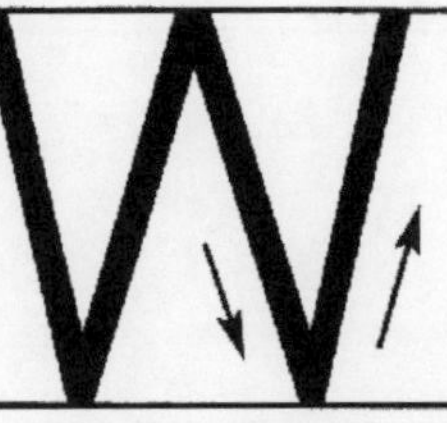

slide down and up

Start on the dot. Trace and copy **W**.

worms

Start at the top!

down
bump

cross

Start on the dot. Trace and copy t.

top

Start on the dot. Trace Tt.

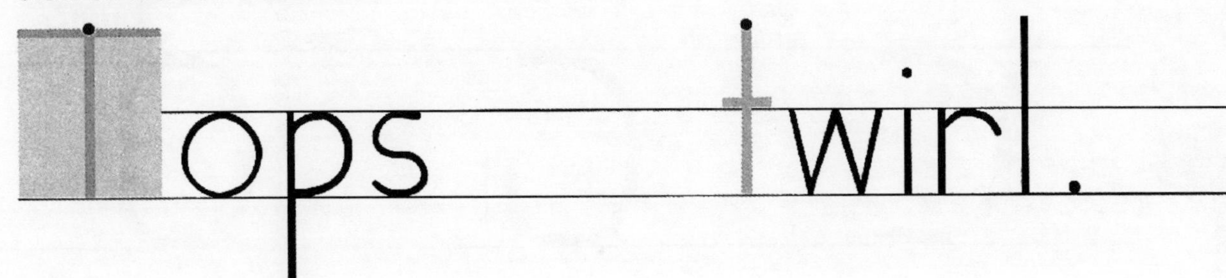

Tops twirl.

Start on the dot. Trace Vv.

V is for van.

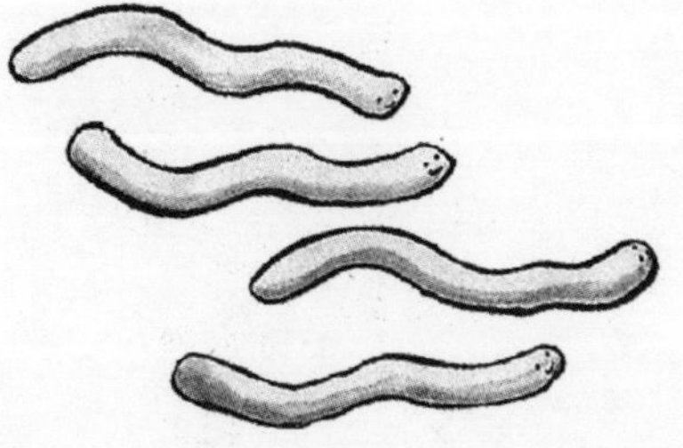

Start on the dot. Trace Ww.

Worms wiggle.

bump

Magic c

up like a

back down
bump

Start on the dot. Trace and copy a.

A a a a a a a a

apple

Trace a.

Aa

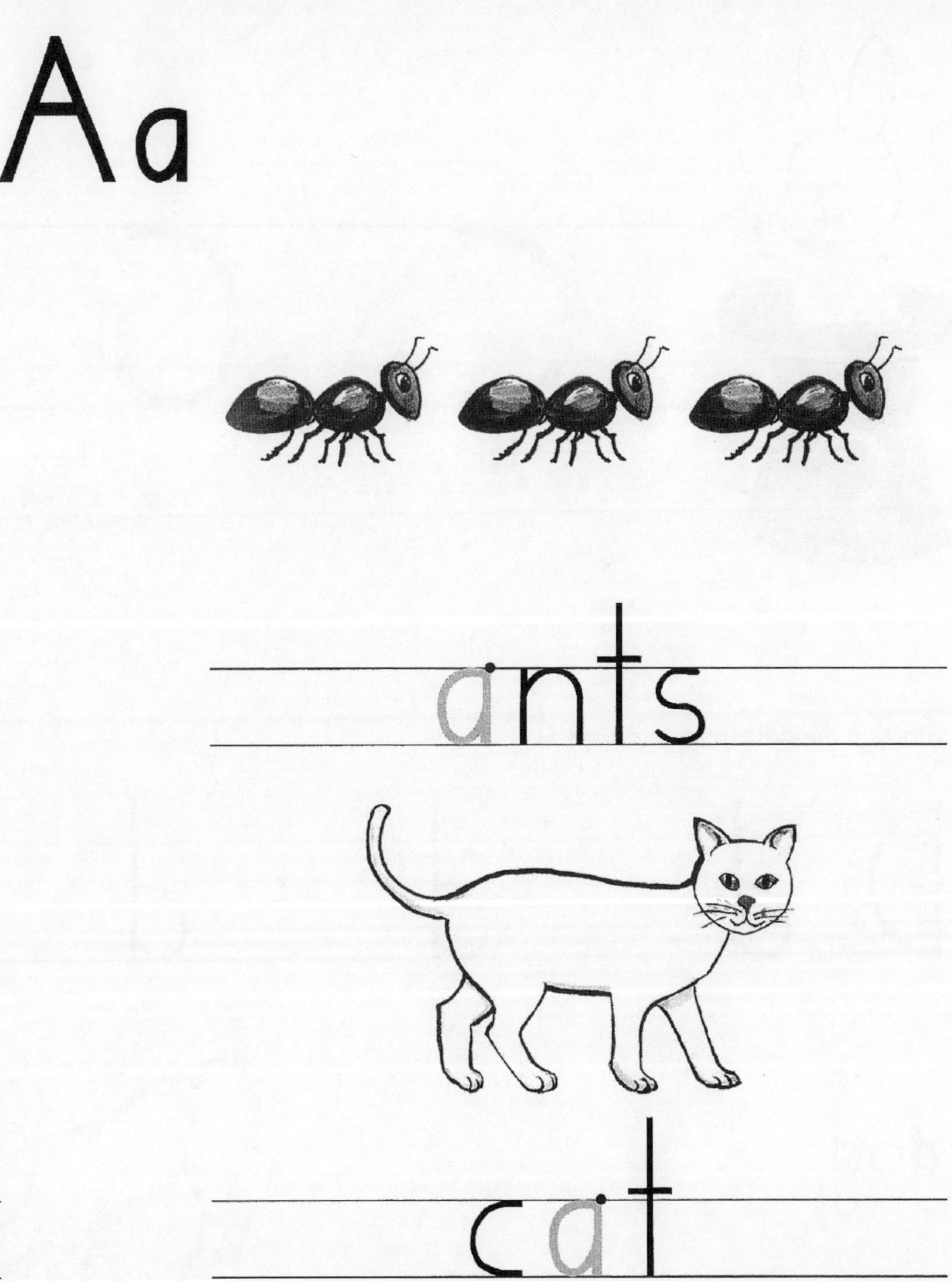

apron

ants

pan

cat

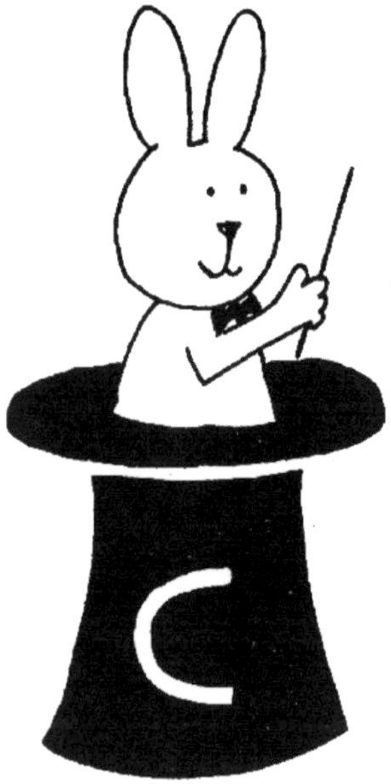

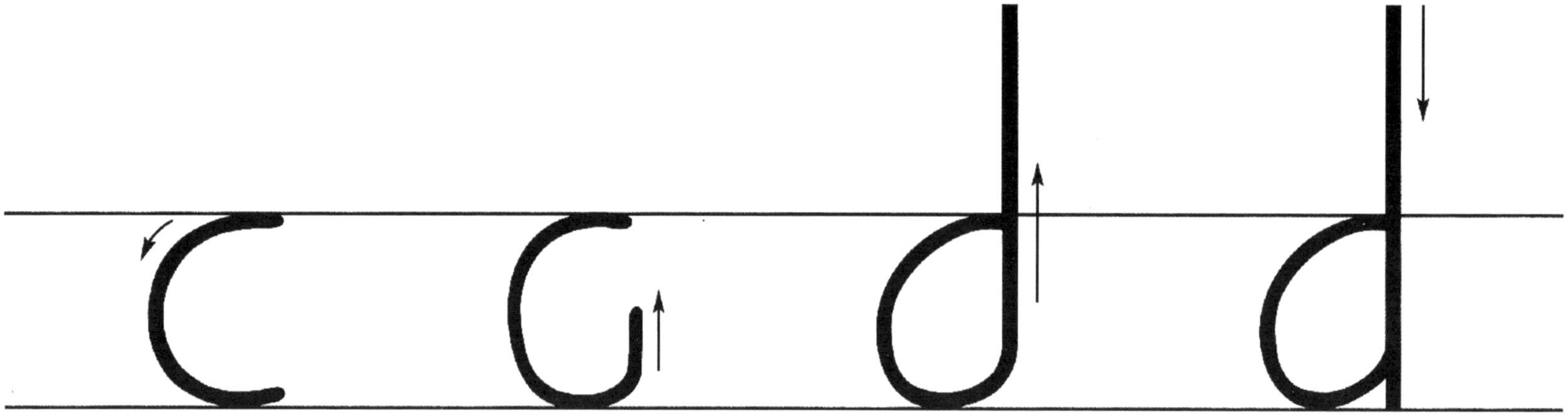

Magic c

up like a

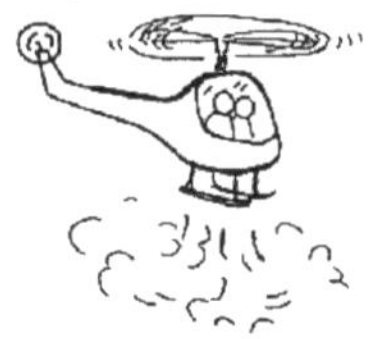

up higher

back down bump

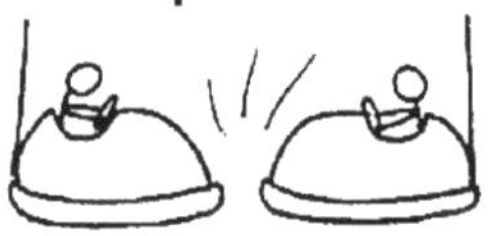

Start on the dot. Trace and copy d.

dog

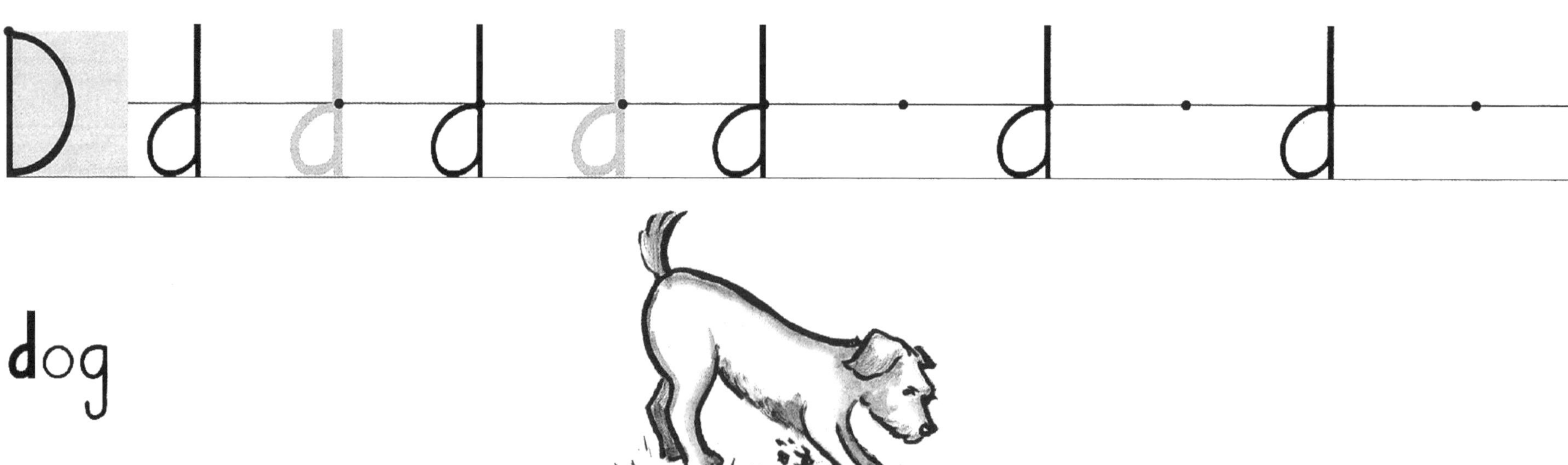

Trace d.

Dd

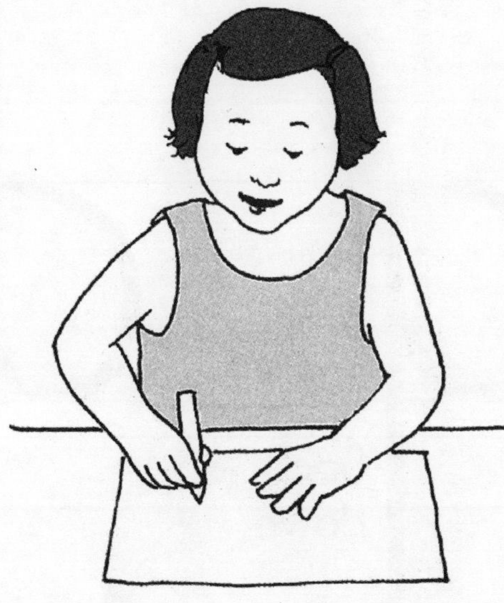

draw

drink

dolphin

duck

bump

c a q g

Magic c

up like a

back down

turn

Start on the dot. Trace and copy g.

G g g g g g g g

goat

Trace g.

Gg

GREEN

green

guitar

grapes

gas

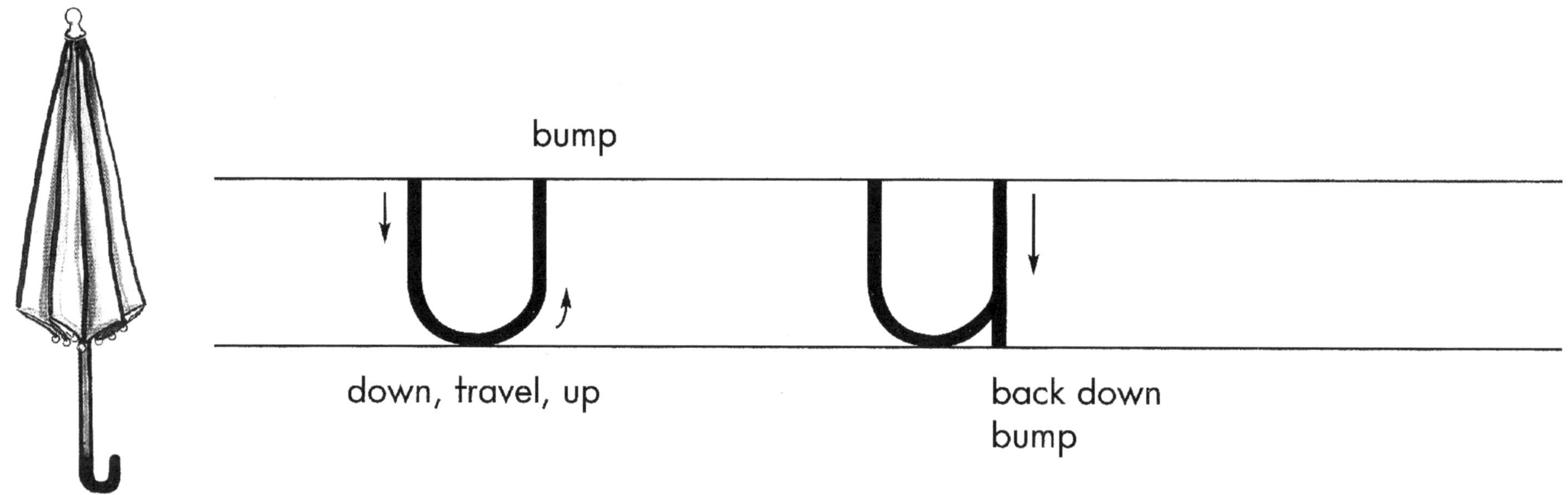

Start on the dot. Trace and copy u.

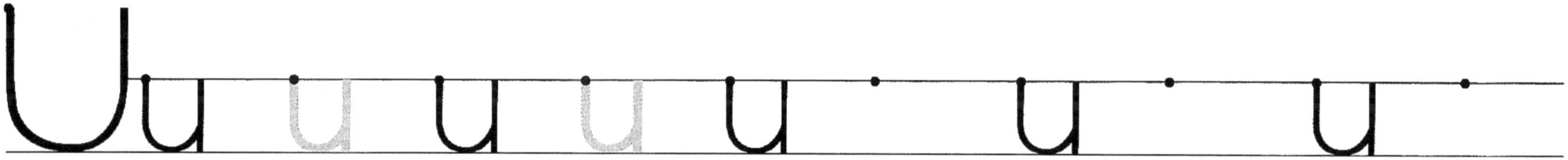

Uu u u u u u u

umbrella

Trace u.

Uu

up

under

skunk

cut

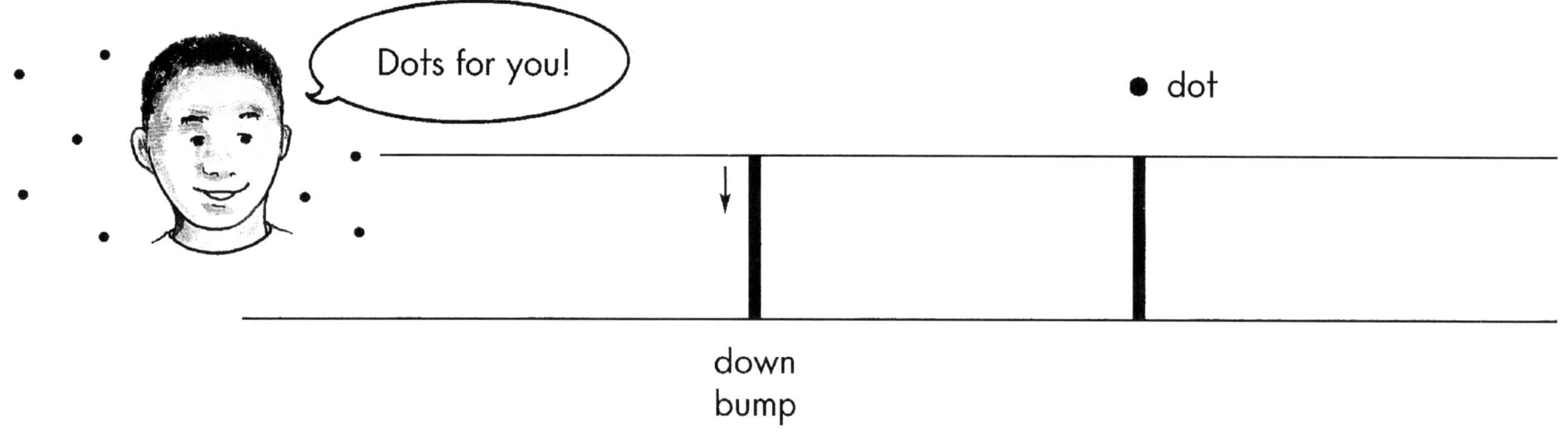

Start on the dot. Trace and copy i.

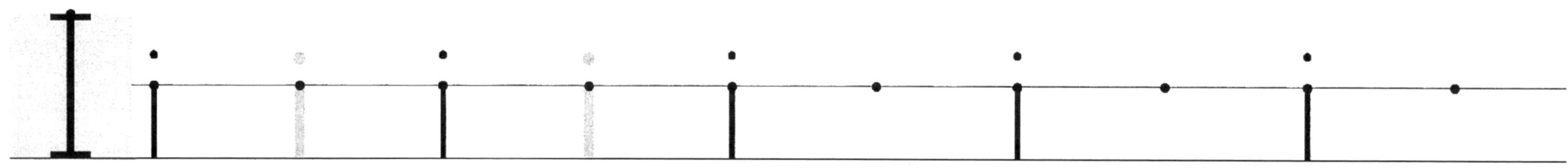

igloo

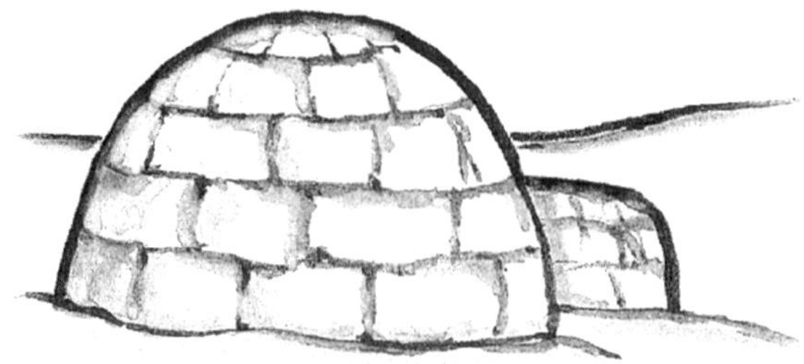

Trace i.

ice

inches

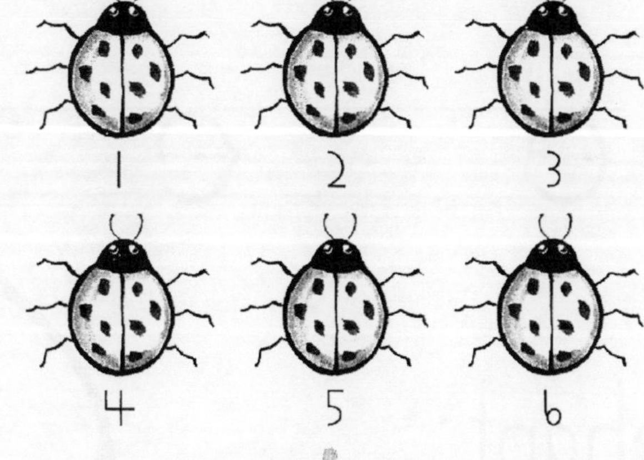

pig

six

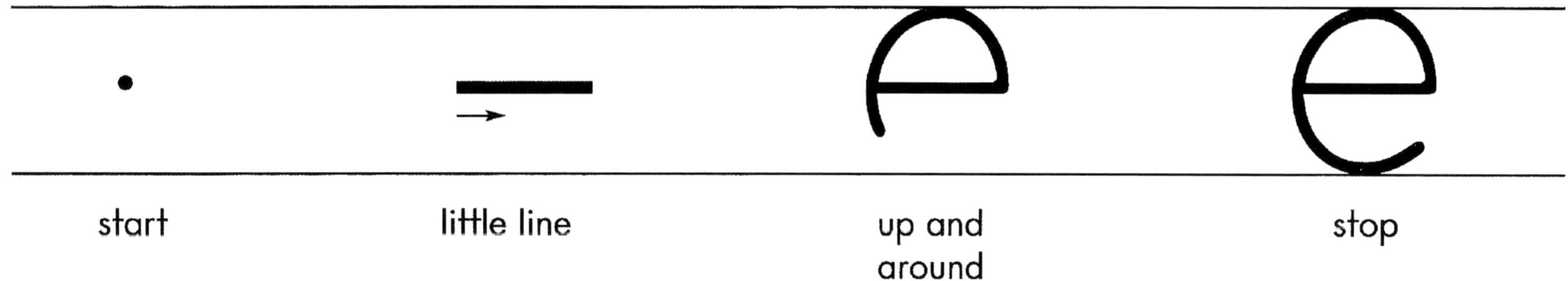

Start on the dot. Trace and copy e.

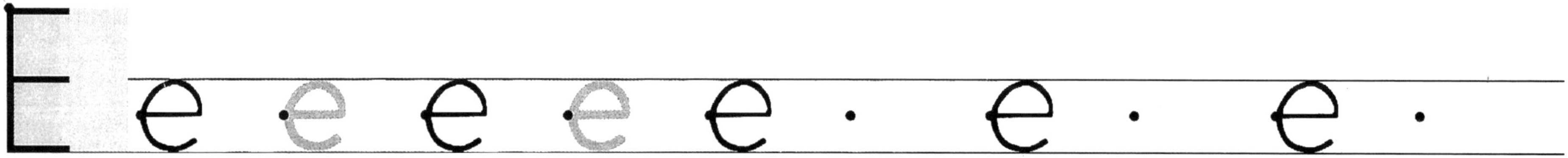

E e e e e e e e

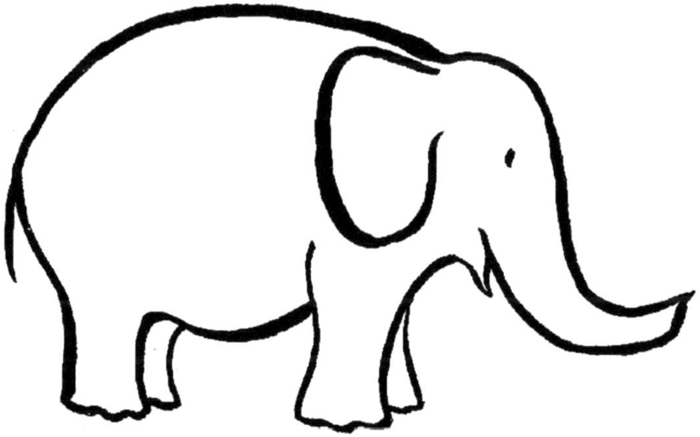

elephant

Trace e.

E e

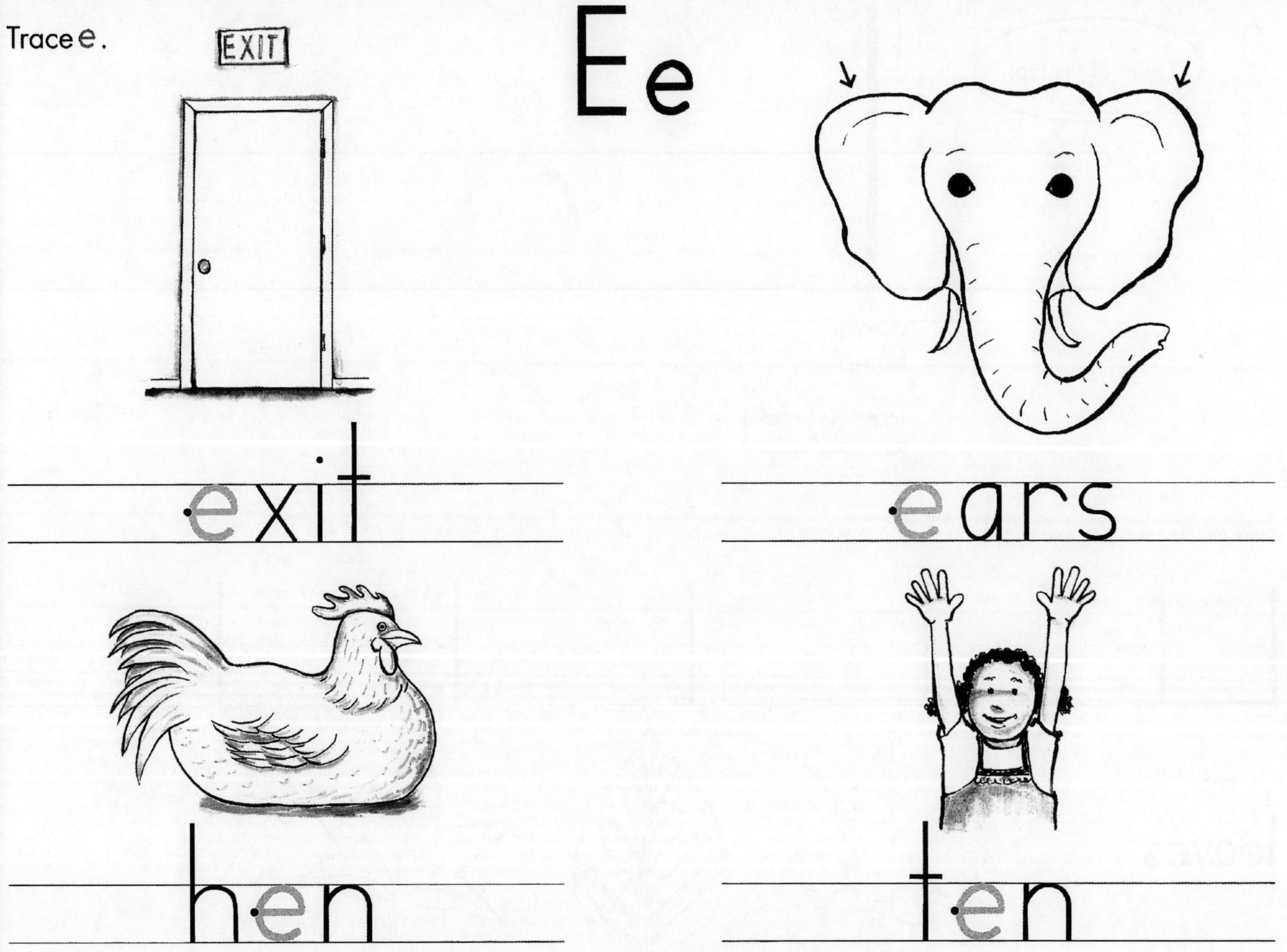

Start at the top!

down
bump

Start on the dot. Trace and copy l.

leaves

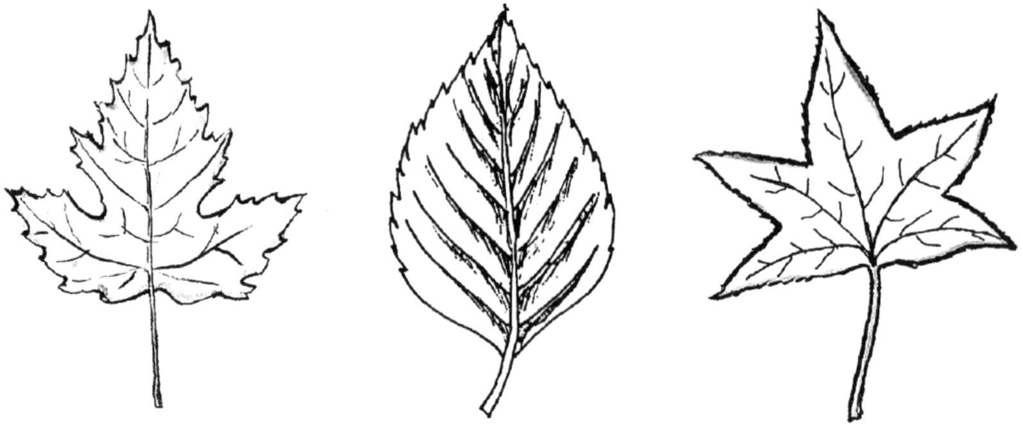

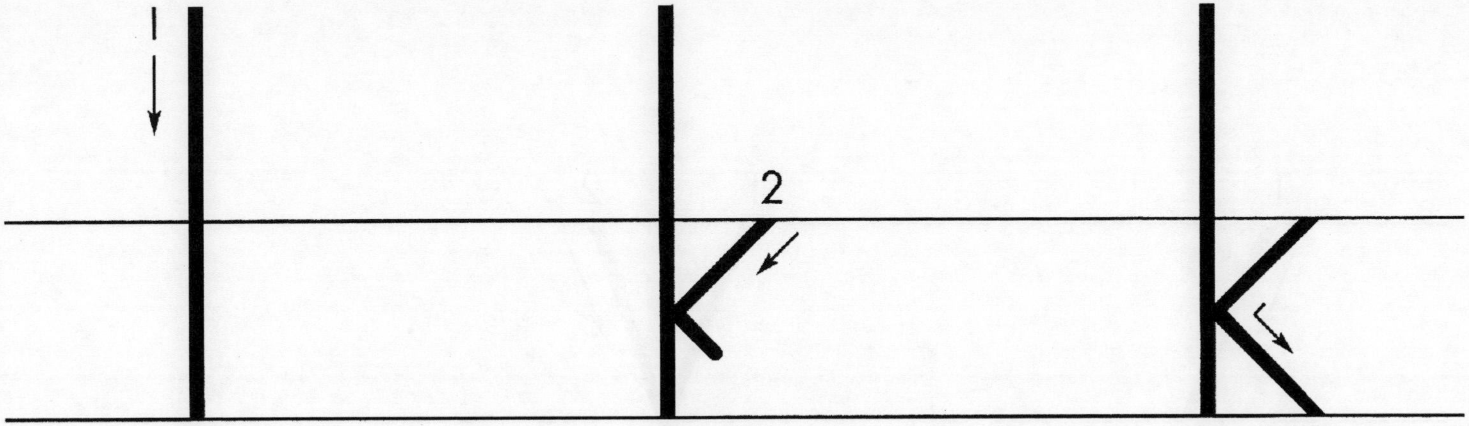

down
bump

kick!

slide away

Start on the dot. Trace and copy k.

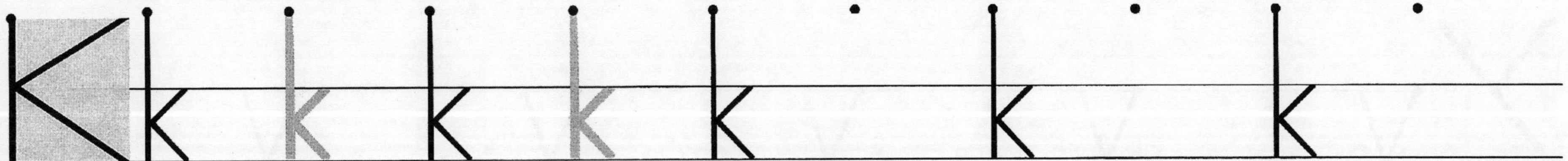

kangaroo

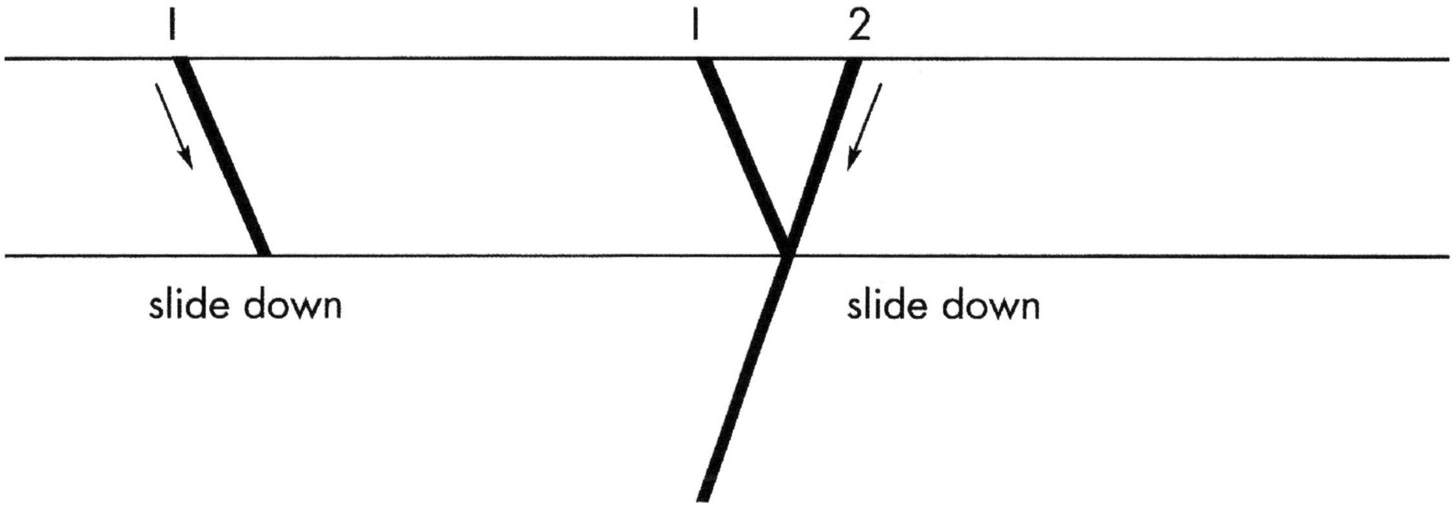

1

slide down

1 2

y

slide down

Start on the dot. Trace and copy y.

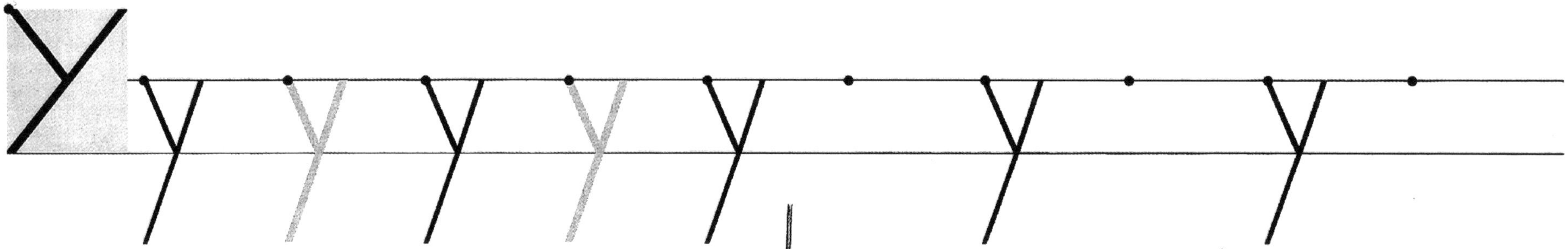

y y y y y y y y

yo-yo

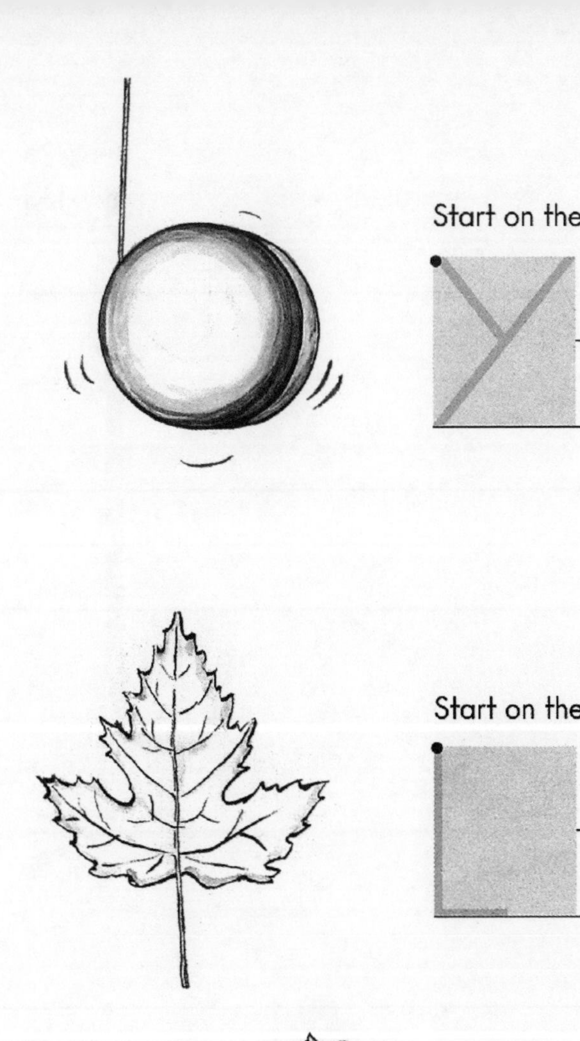

Start on the dot. Trace Yy.

Start on the dot. Trace Ll.

Start on the dot. Trace Kk.

Kangaroos kick.

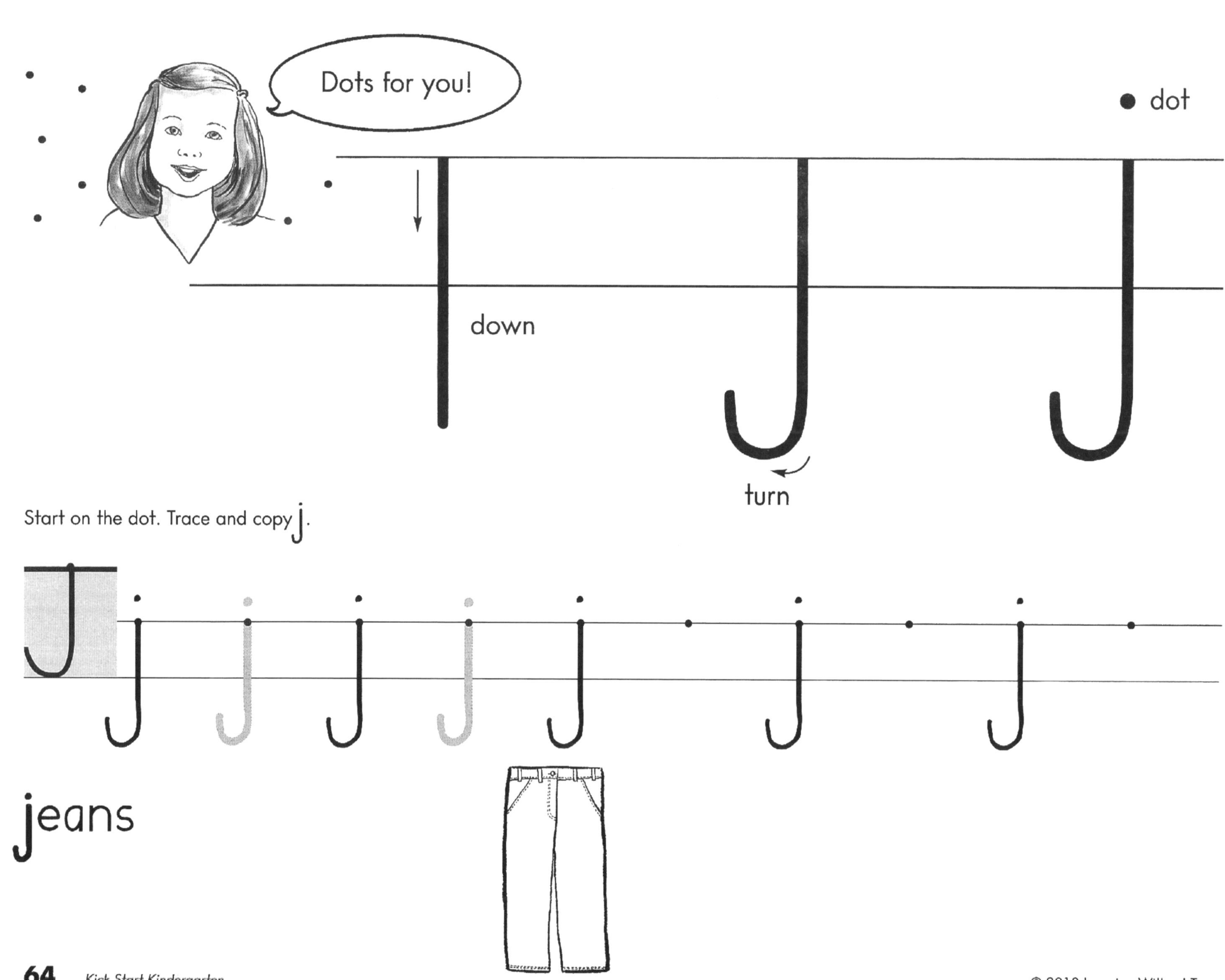

Dots for you!
dot
down
turn
Start on the dot. Trace and copy j.
jeans

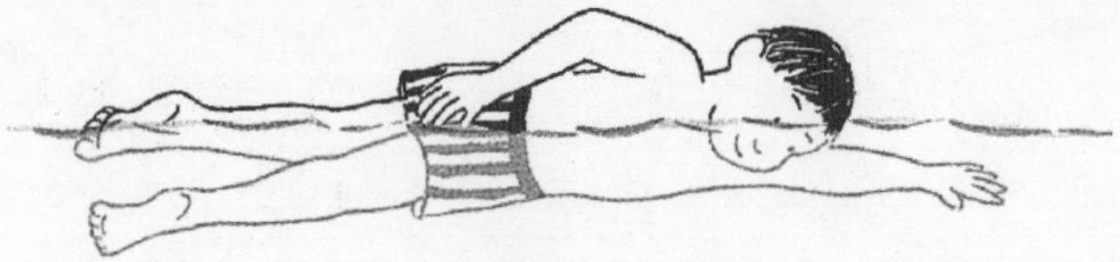

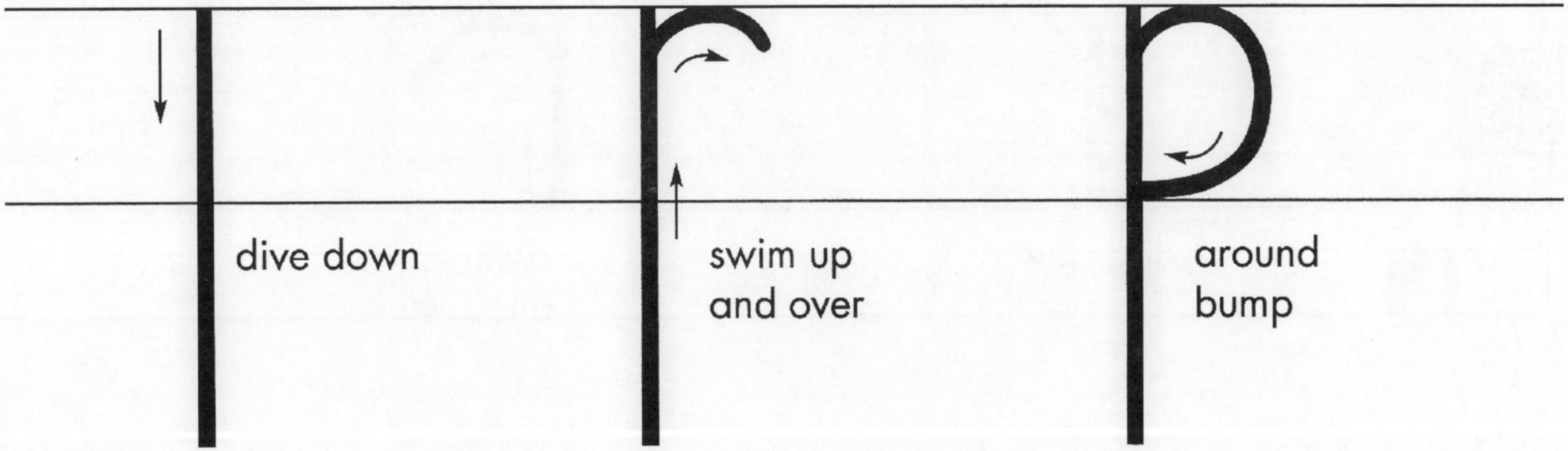

dive down

swim up
and over

around
bump

Start on the dot. Trace and copy p.

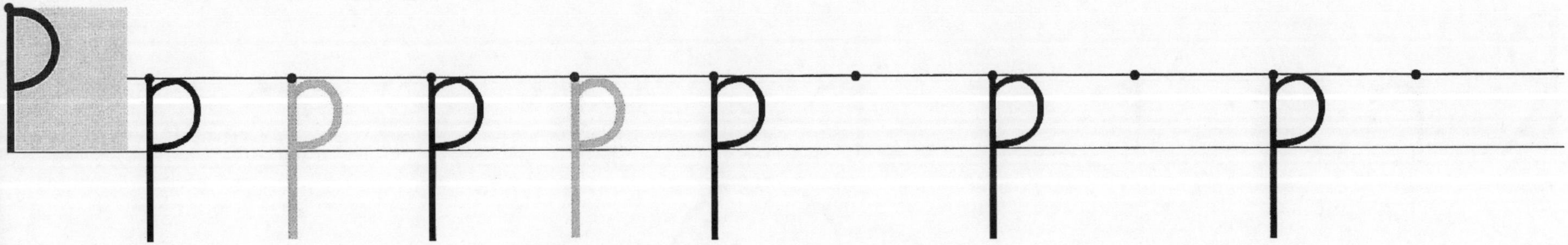

p p p p p p p p

puppies

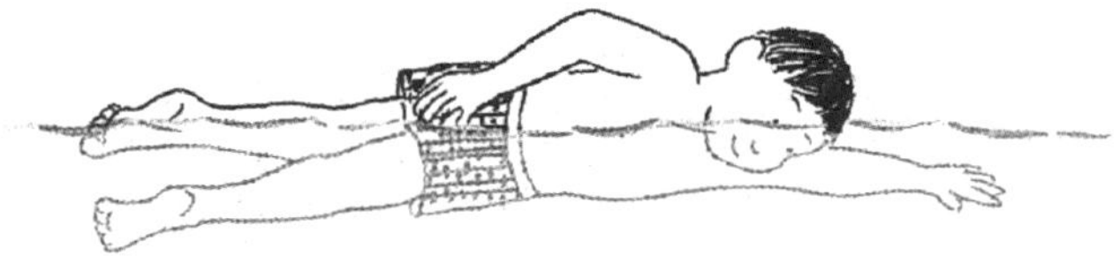

dive down

swim up
and over

Start on the dot. Trace and copy r.

R r r r r r r r

rain

Start on the dot. Trace Rr.

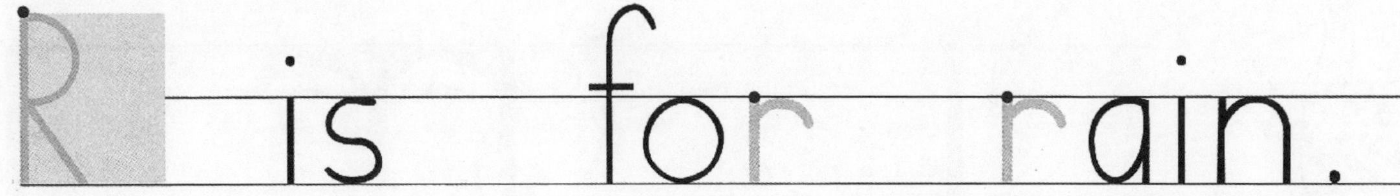

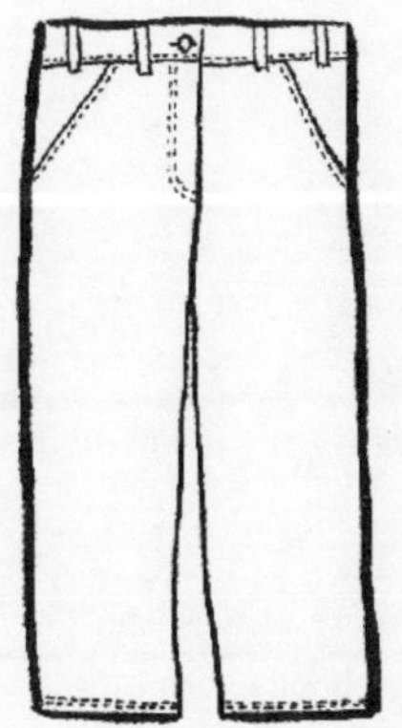

Start on the dot. Trace Jj.

Start on the dot. Trace Pp.

Puppies play.

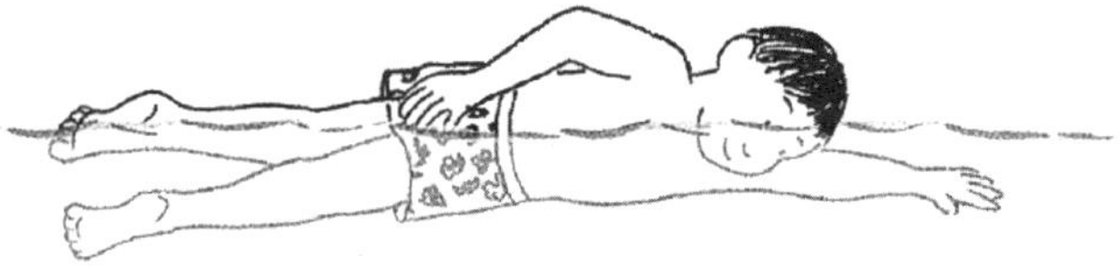

dive down

swim up
and over

down

Start on the dot. Trace and copy n.

Nn n n n n n n

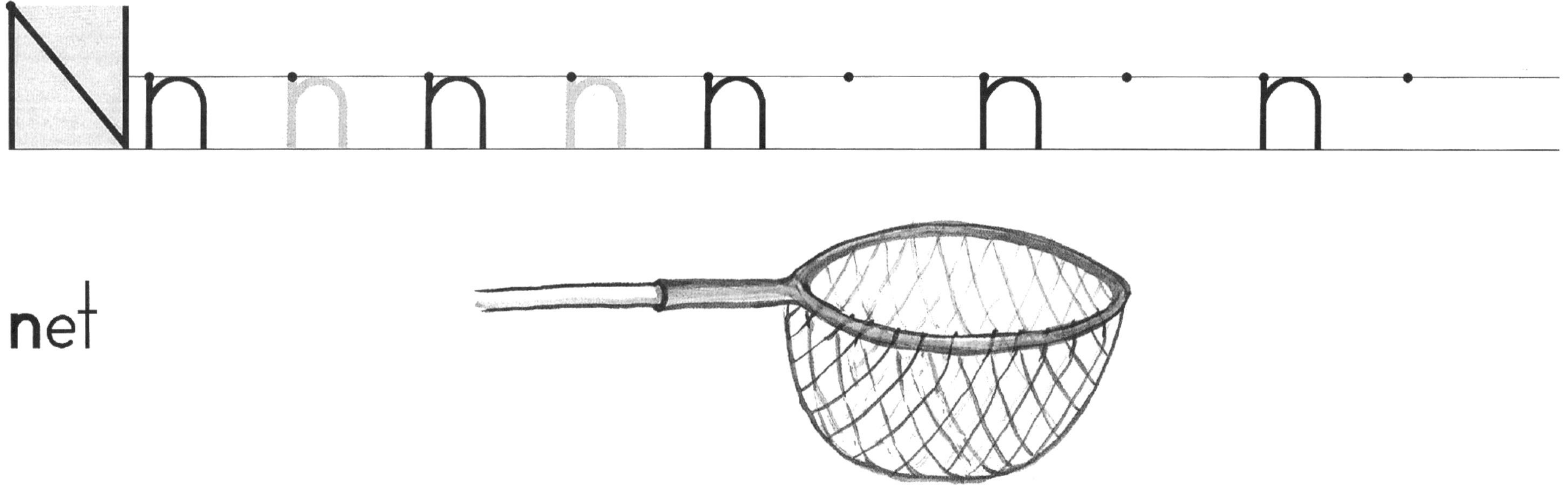

net

Trace n.

Nn

night

nose

nail

neck

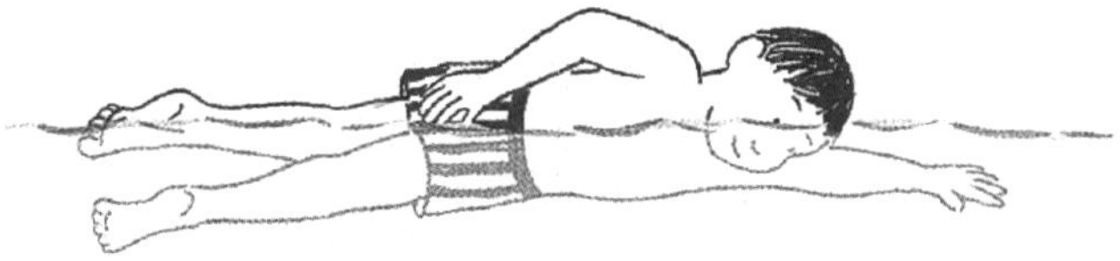

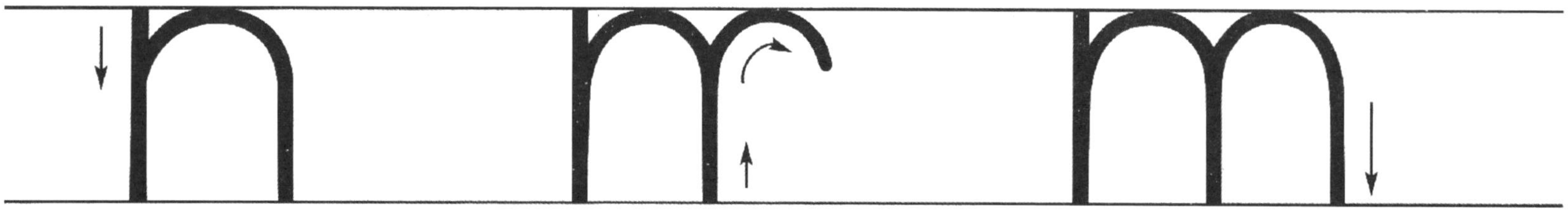

n m m

start with n

swim up
and over

down

Start on the dot. Trace and copy m.

Mm m m m m m m

moon

Trace m.

Mm

mouse

moose

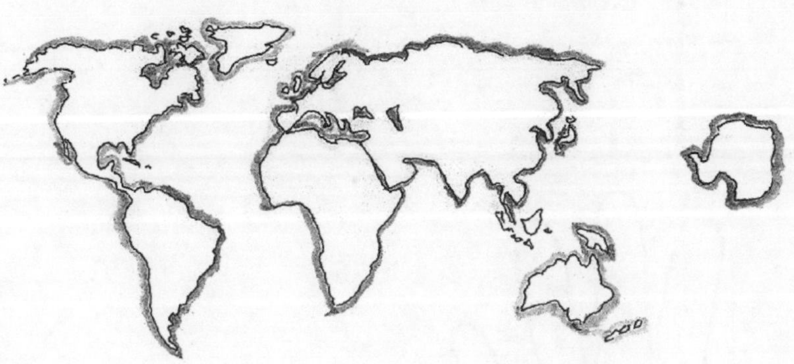

map

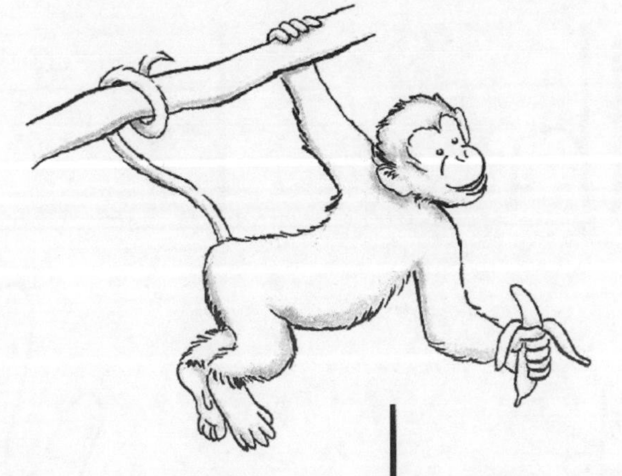

monkey

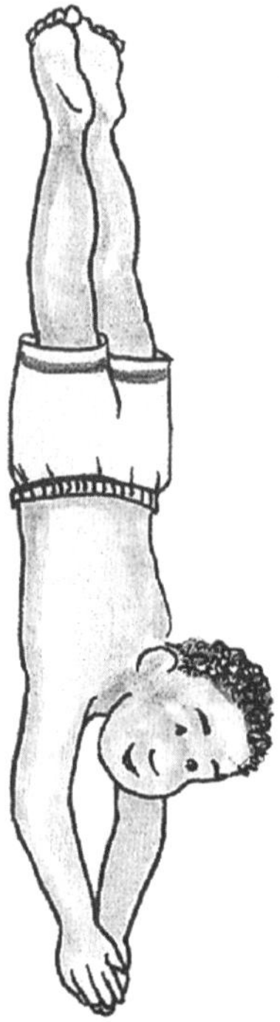

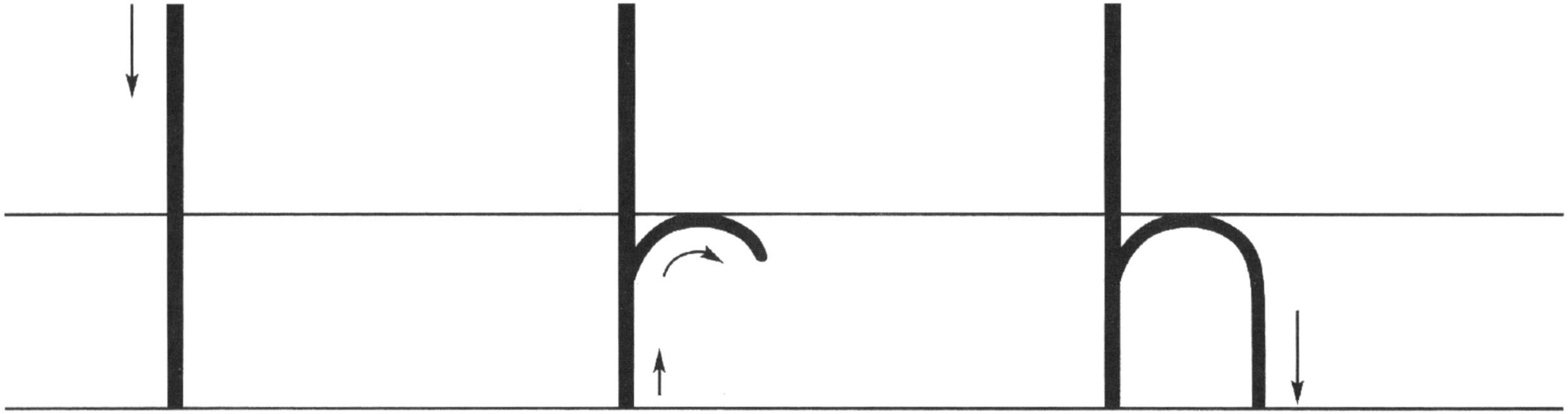

dive down

swim up
and over

down

Start on the dot. Trace and copy h.

Hh h h h h h h

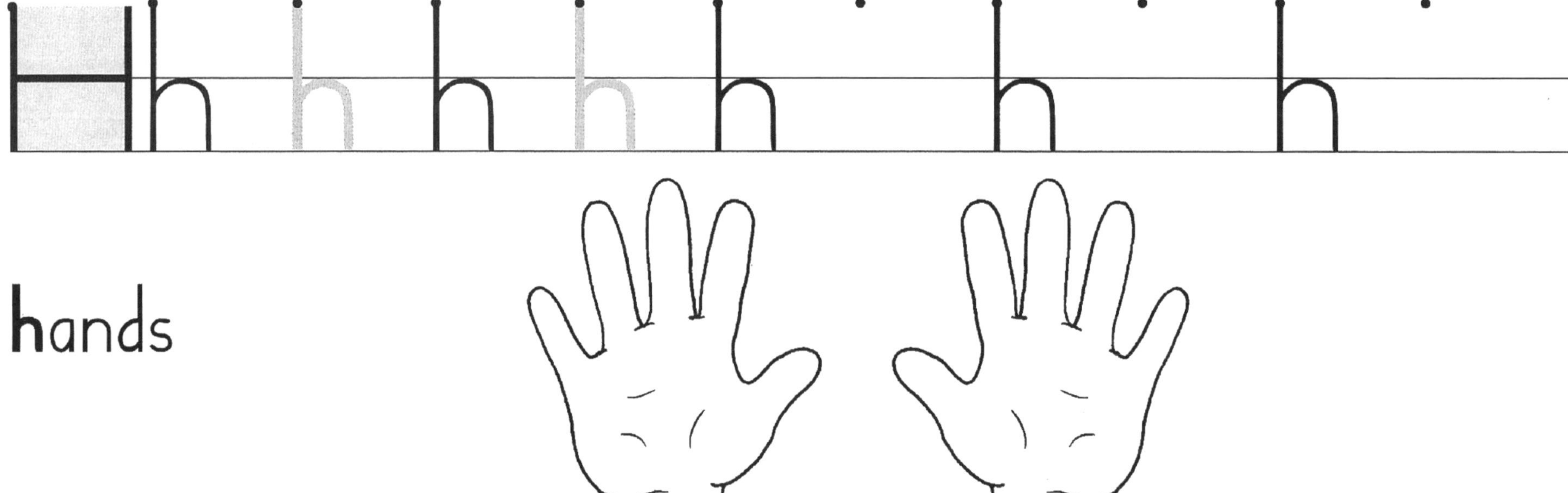

hands

Trace h.

Hh

hat

hop

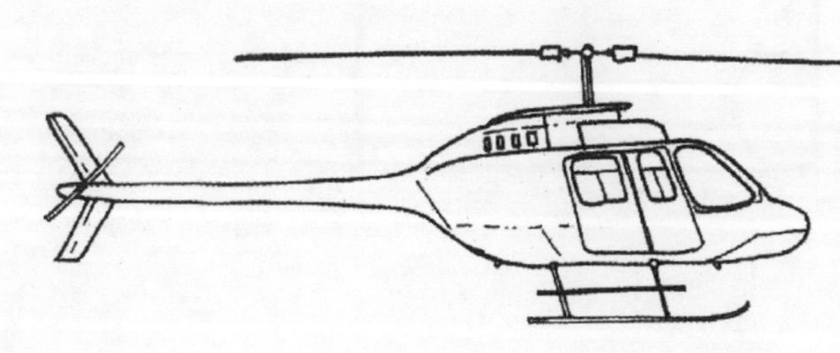

hippo

helicopter

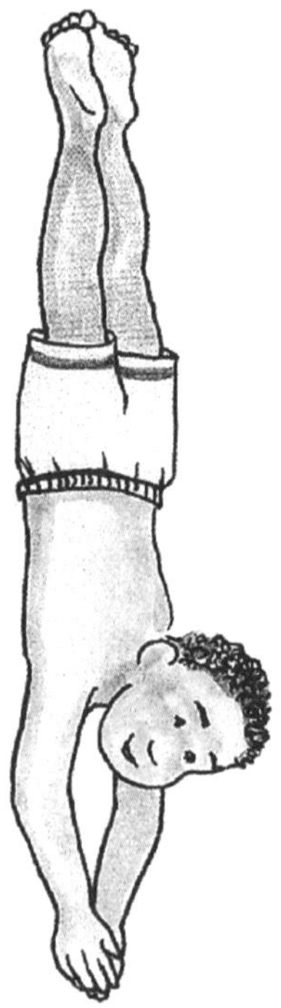

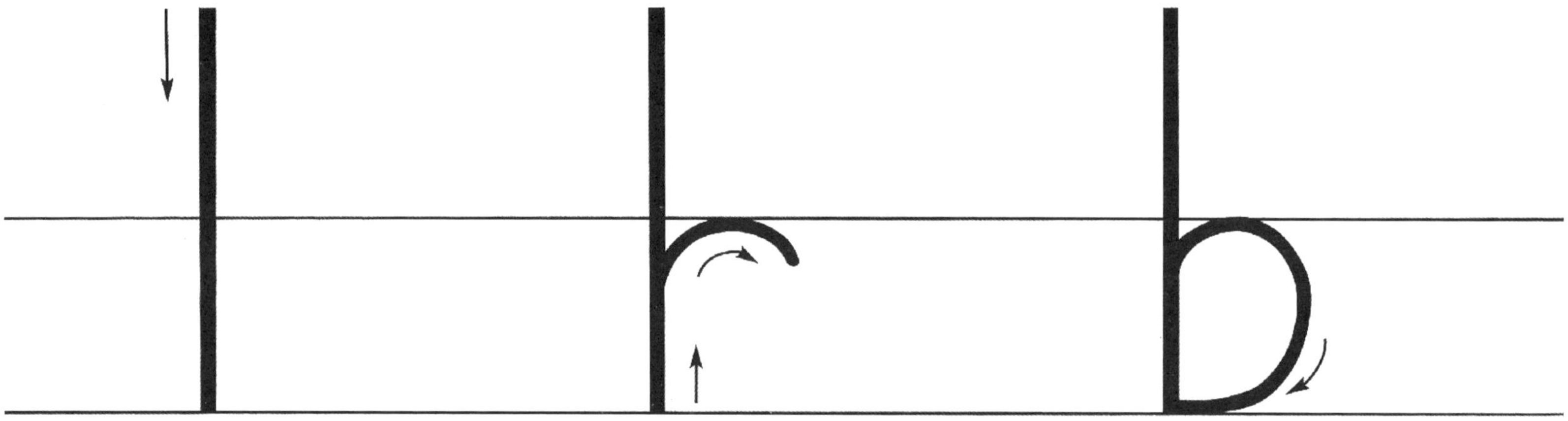

dive down

swim up
and over

around
bump

Start on the dot. Trace and copy b.

B b b b b b b b

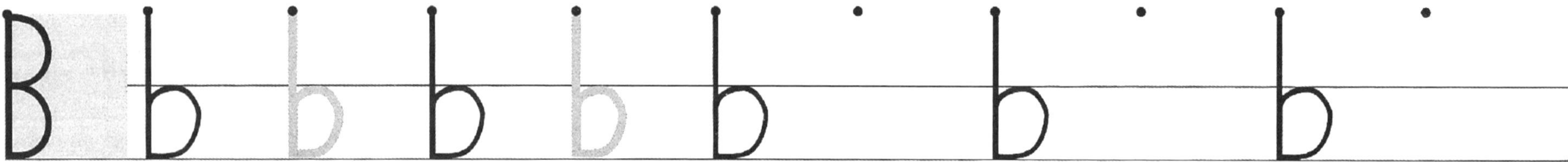

bear

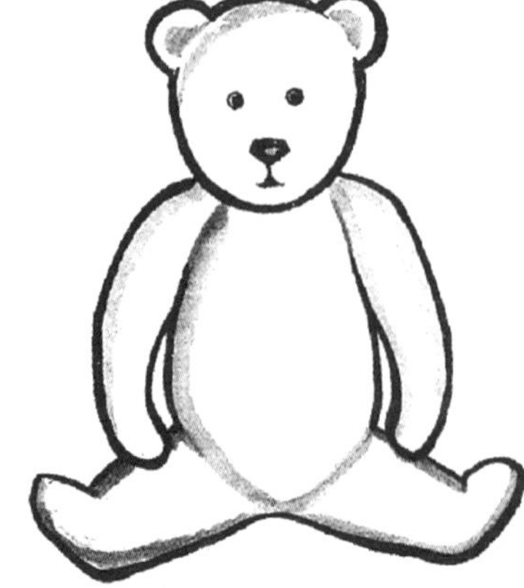

Trace b.

Bb

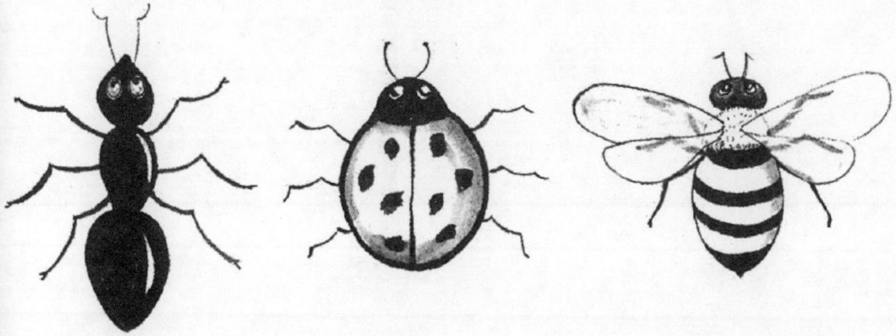

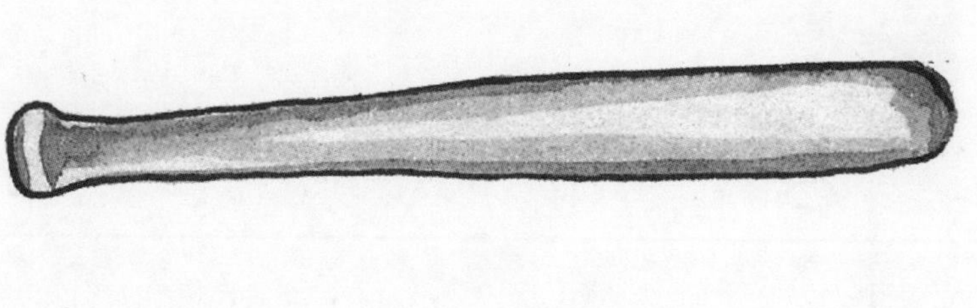

bugs

bat

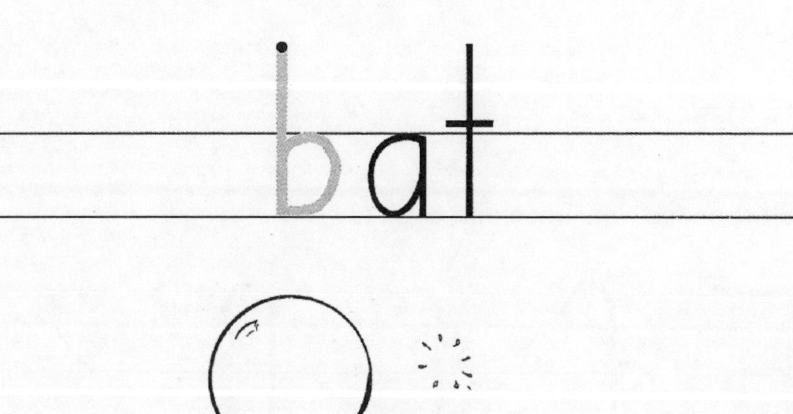

baby

bubbles

At first, curve up.
Then, go straight down.

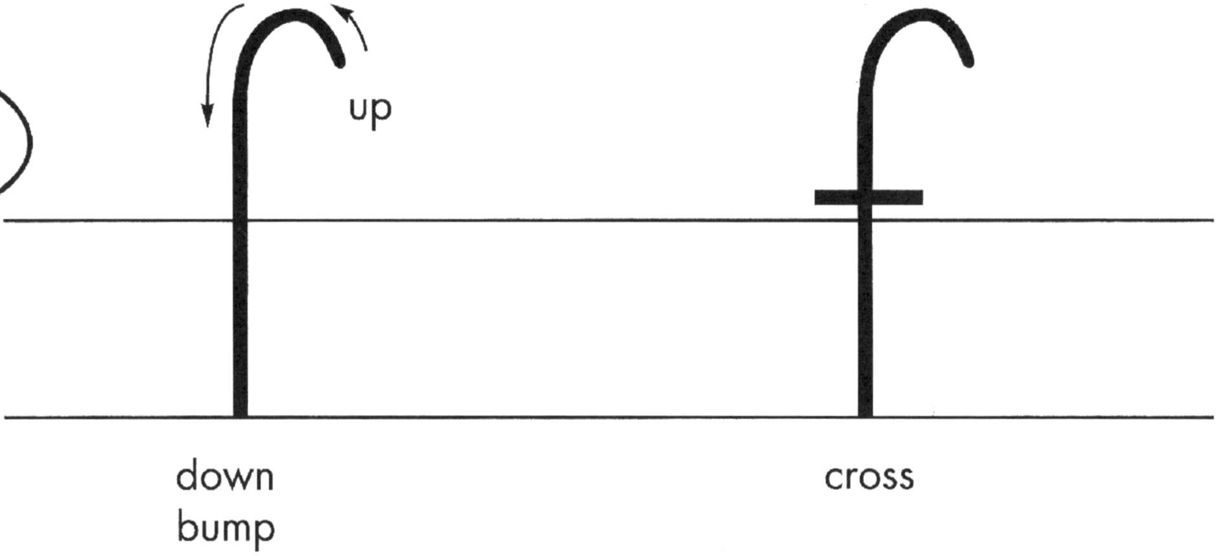

up

down
bump

cross

Start on the dot. Trace and copy f.

F f f f f f f f

firetruck

Trace f.

Ff

fish

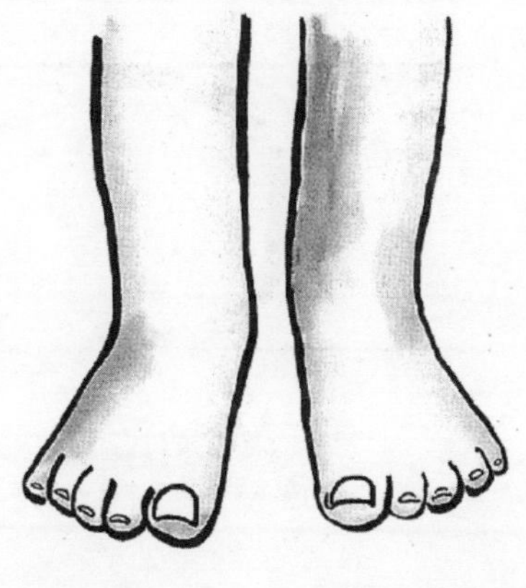

feet

flower

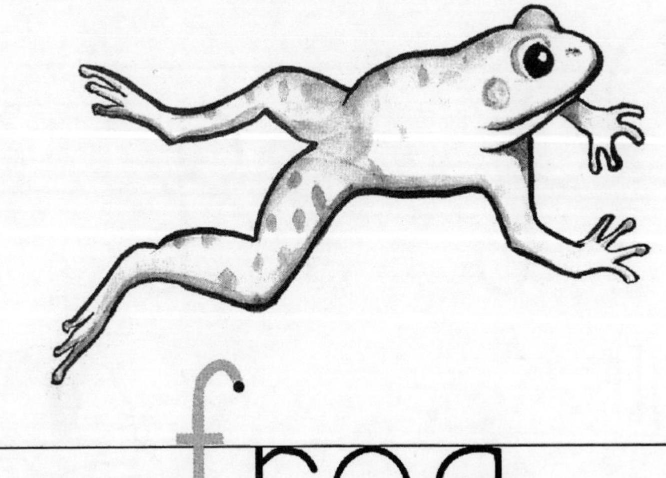

frog

bump

Magic c

up like a

back down

U-turn

Start on the dot. Trace and copy q.

Q q q q q q q q

quilt

slide down   slide down

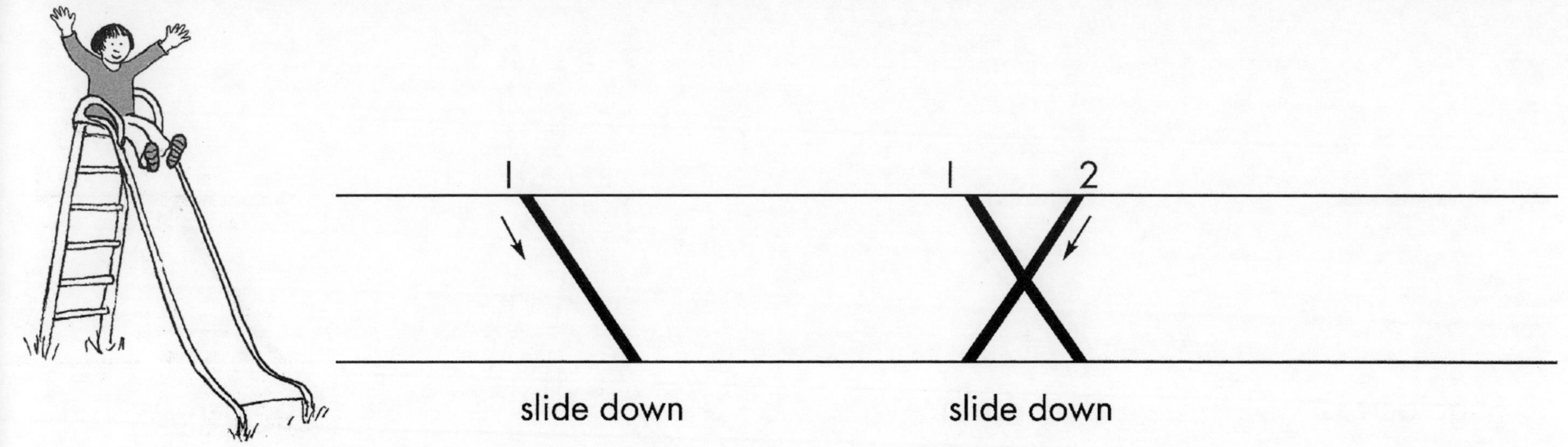

Start on the dot. Trace and copy **X**.

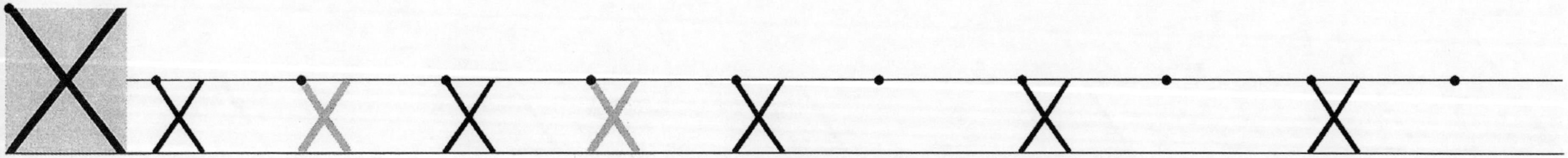

x-ray fish

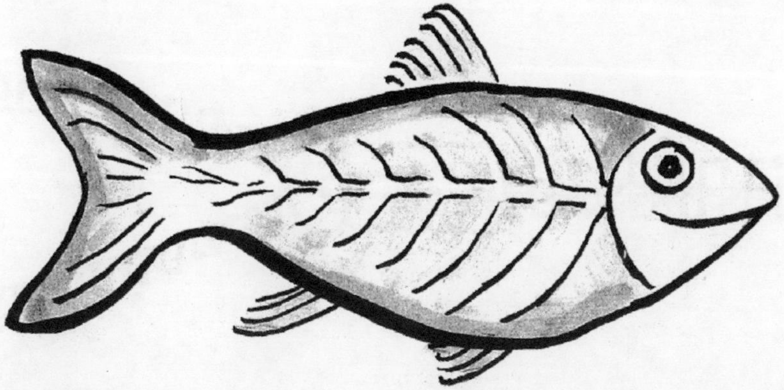

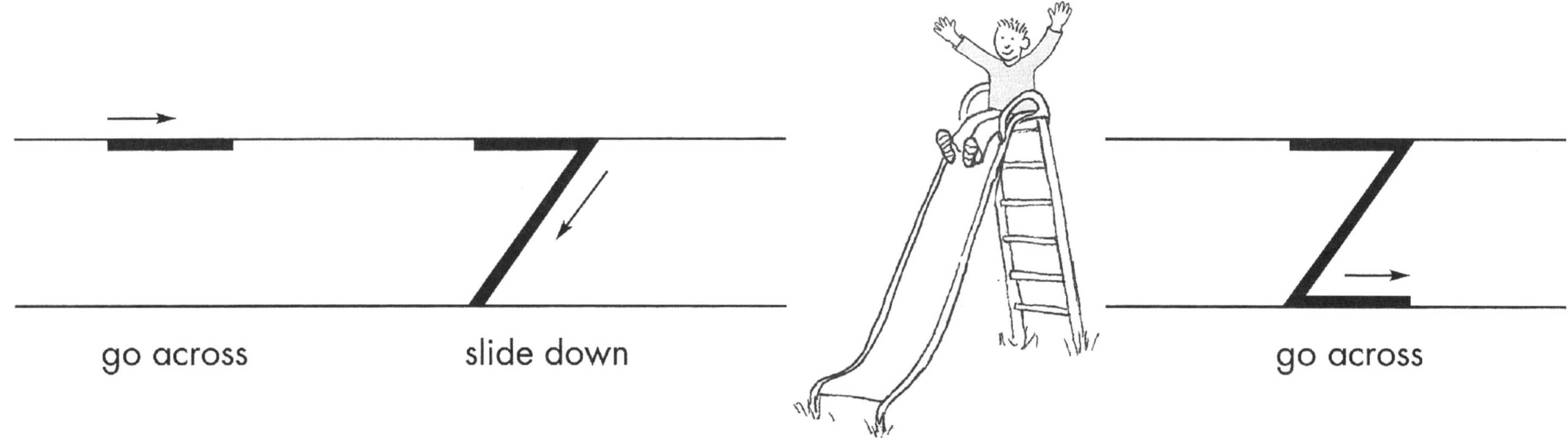

Start on the dot. Trace and copy Z.

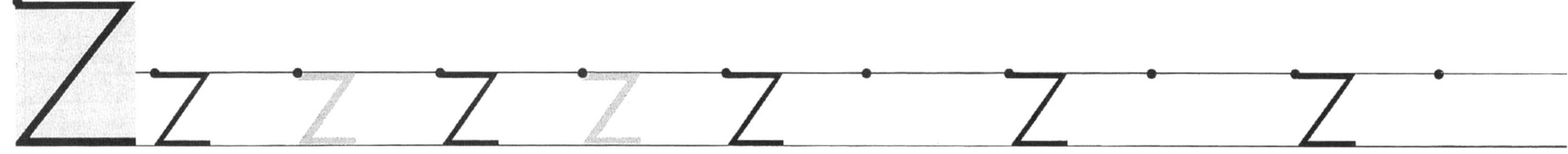

zipper

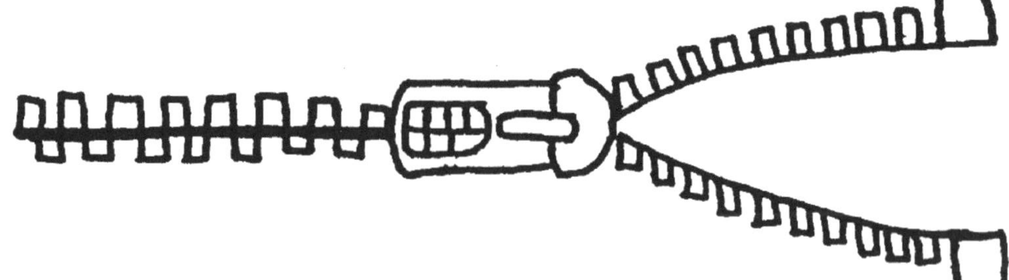

Start on the dot. Trace Z z.

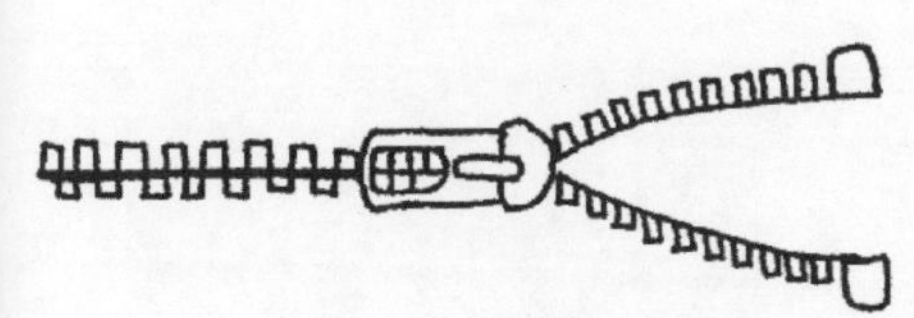

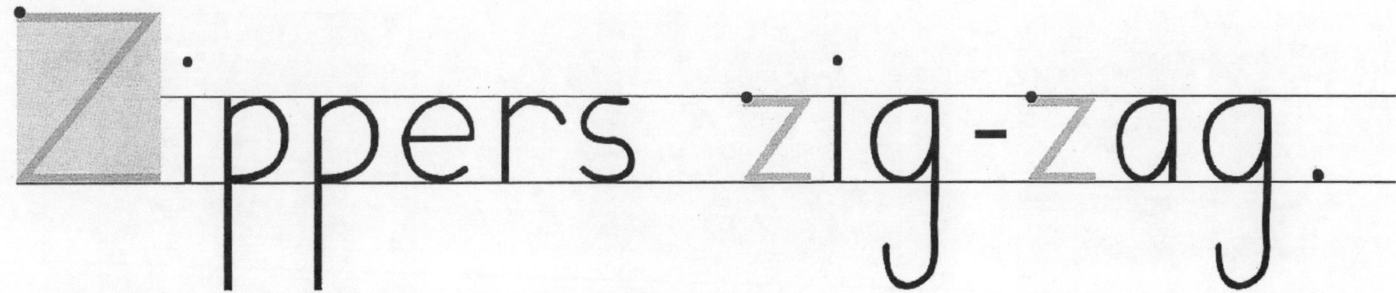

Start on the dot. Trace Q q.

Start on the dot. Trace X x.

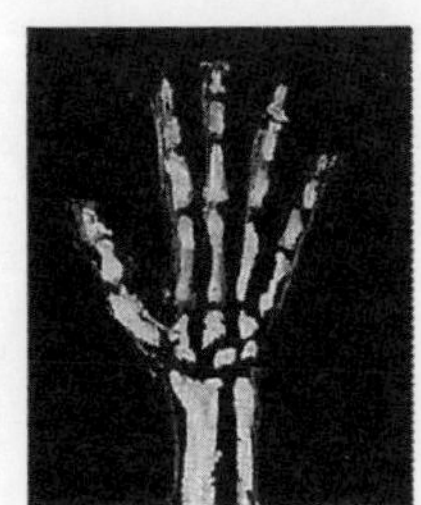

Numbers on the Slate Chalkboard

Teacher writes 4 with chalk.

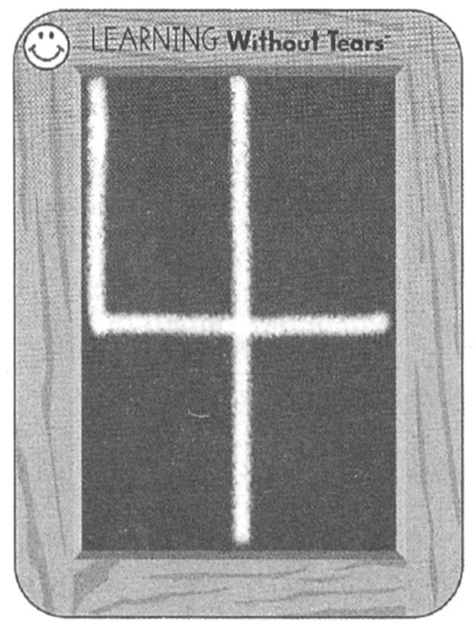

Child wets 4 with a little sponge.

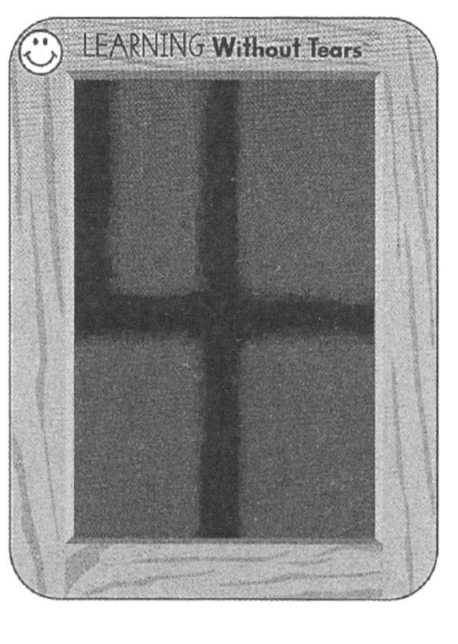

WET

Child dries 4 with a paper towel.

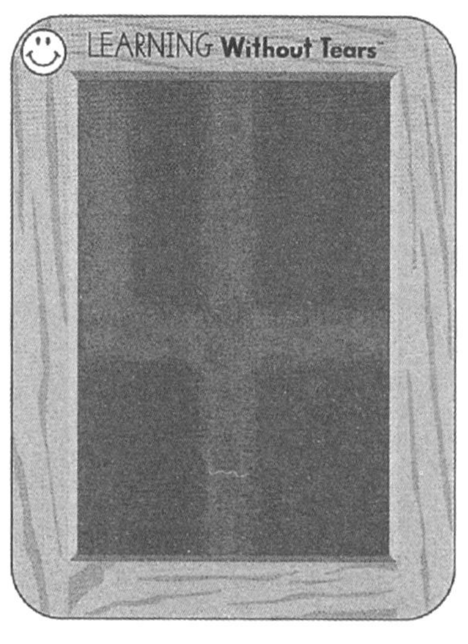

DRY

Child writes 4 with chalk.

TRY

Numbers on Gray Blocks

1 2 3 4 5 6 7 8 9 10

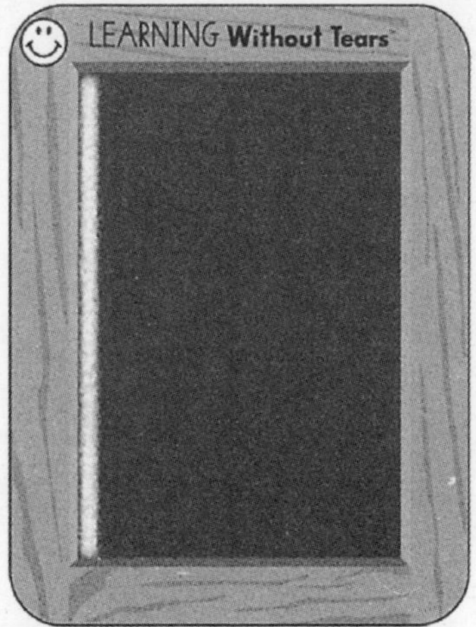

BIG LINE

one

Trace.

Copy.

1 flamingo

2

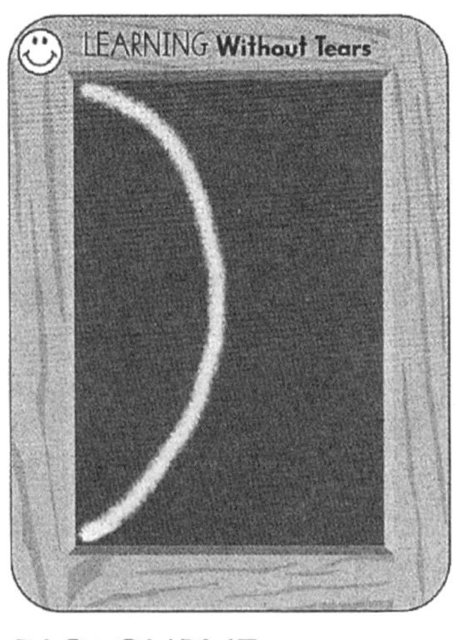

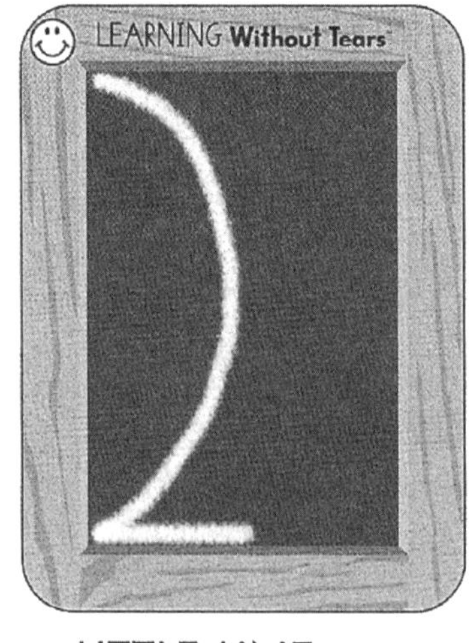

BIG CURVE + LITTLE LINE

two

Trace.

Copy.

2 chicks

3

three

LITTLE CURVE + LITTLE CURVE

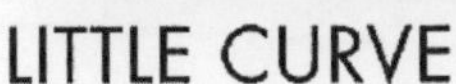

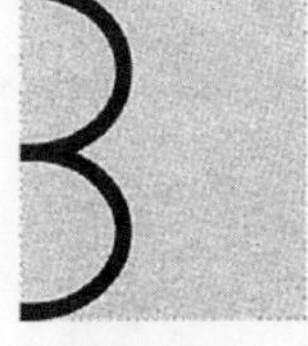

Trace.

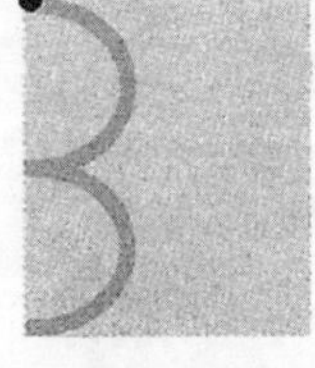

Copy.

3 pigs

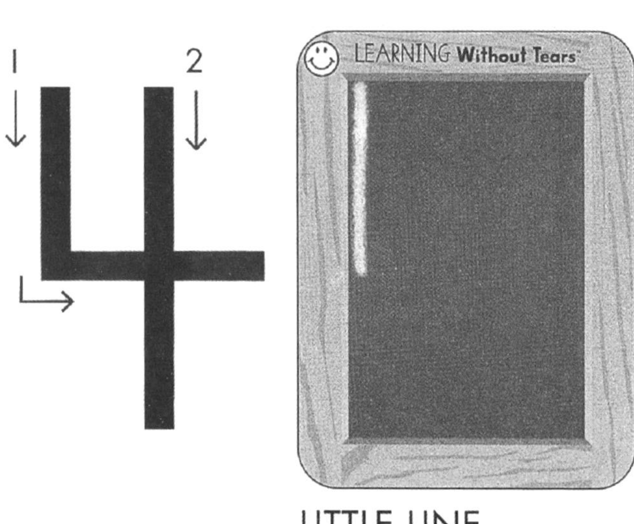

LITTLE LINE

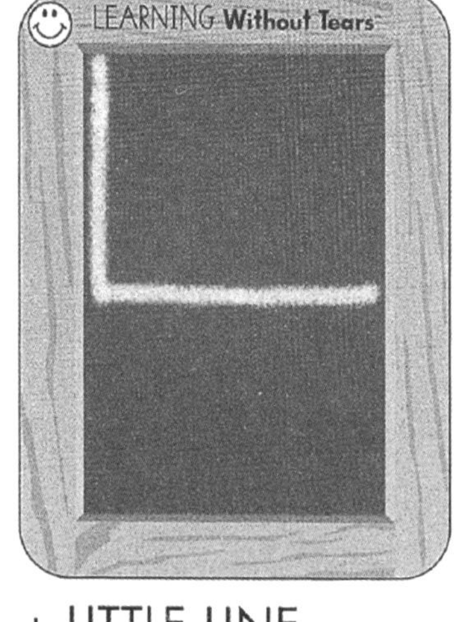

+ LITTLE LINE

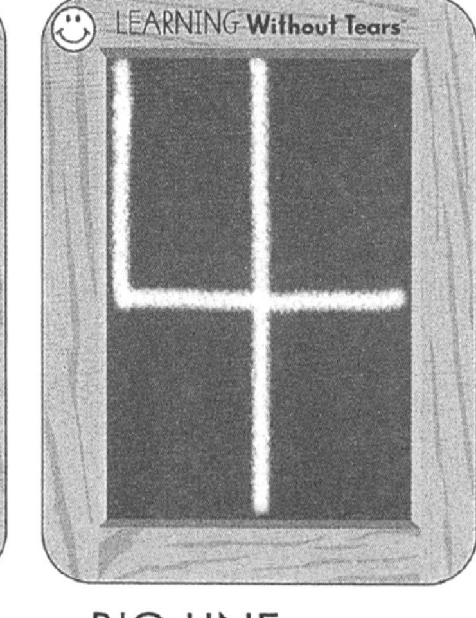

+ BIG LINE

four

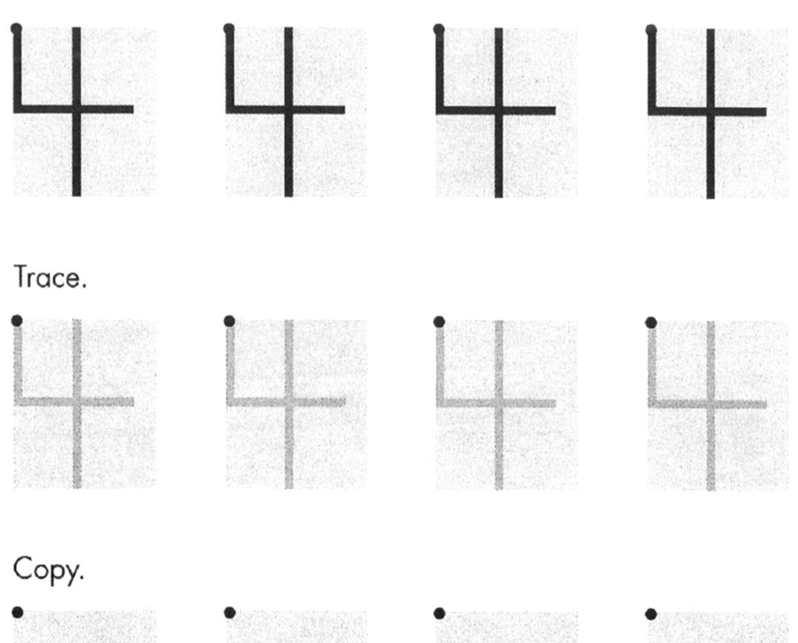

Trace.

Copy.

4 cars

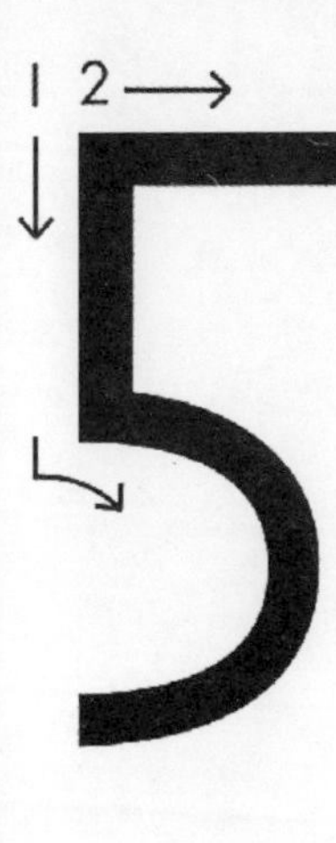

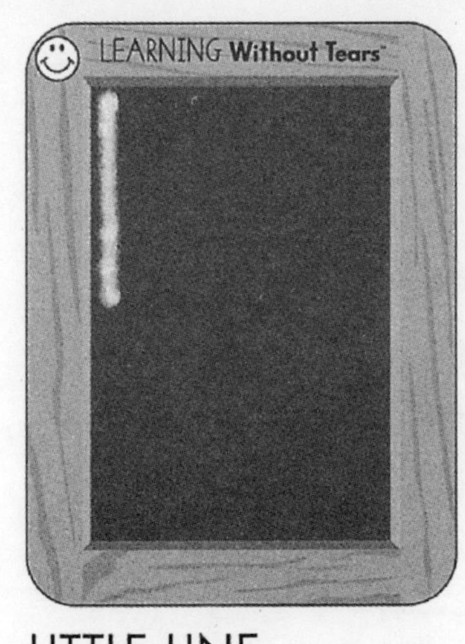

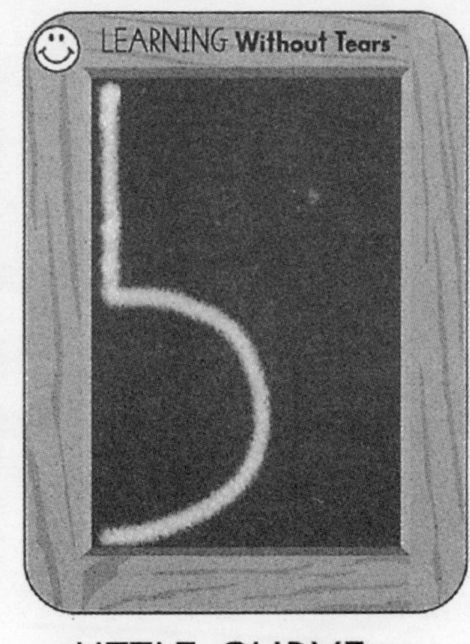

five

LITTLE LINE + LITTLE CURVE + LITTLE LINE

Trace.

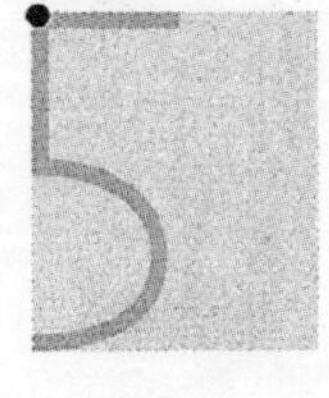

Copy.

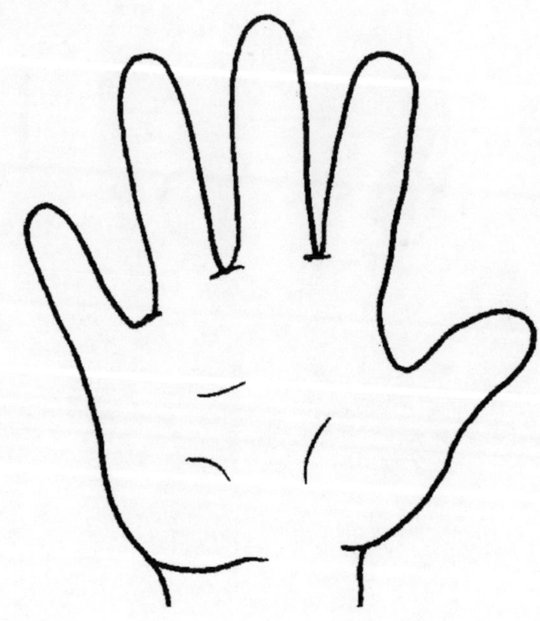

5 fingers

b

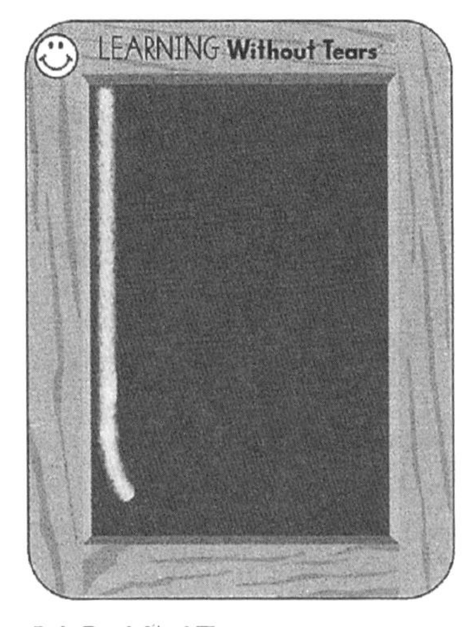

BIG LINE

+ CURL UP IN THE CORNER

six

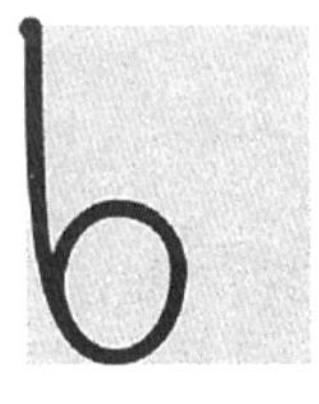

Trace.

Copy.

b bears

→
7

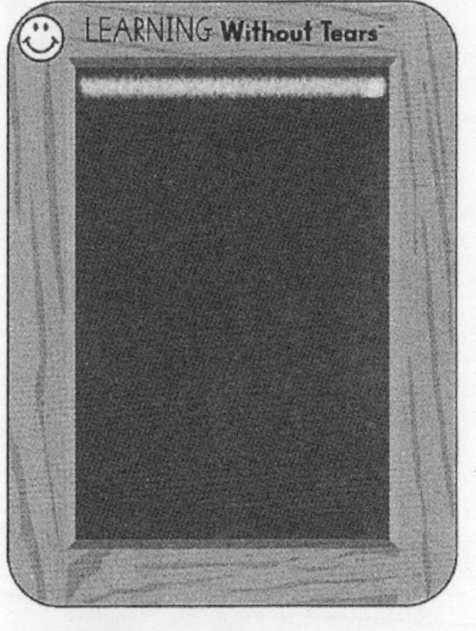

LITTLE LINE

+ BIG LINE

seven

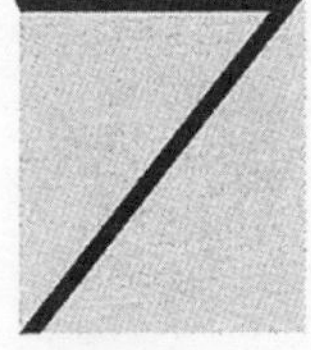   

Trace.

Copy.

7 ducklings

BEGIN WITH S

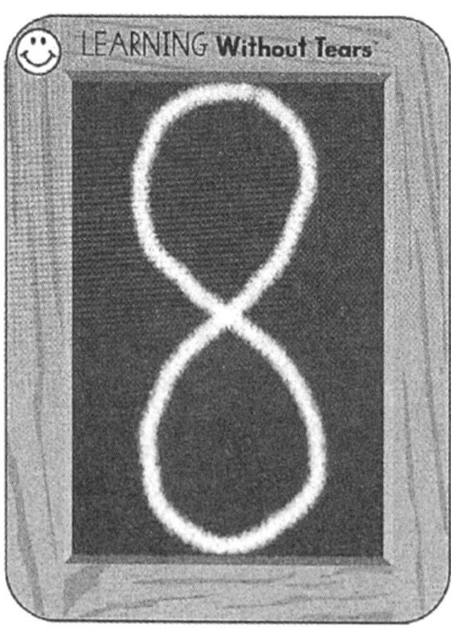

+ UP TO THE TOP

eight

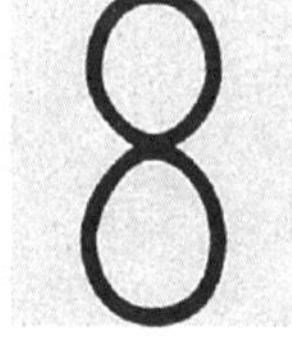 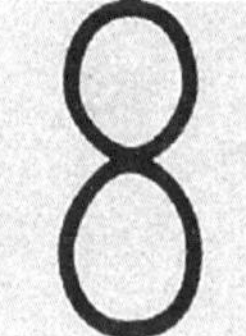 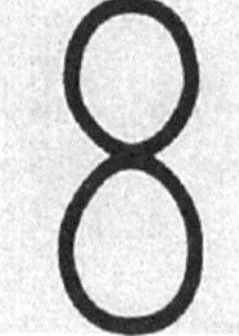 

Trace.

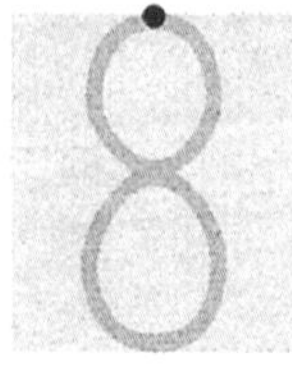 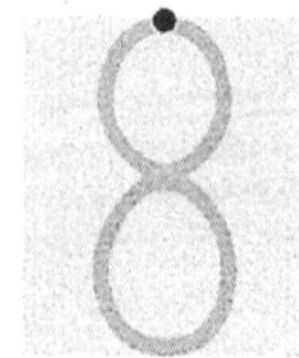 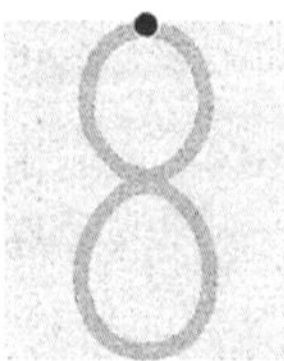 

Copy.

8 octopus arms

LITTLE CURVE + UP + BIG LINE

nine

Trace.

Copy.

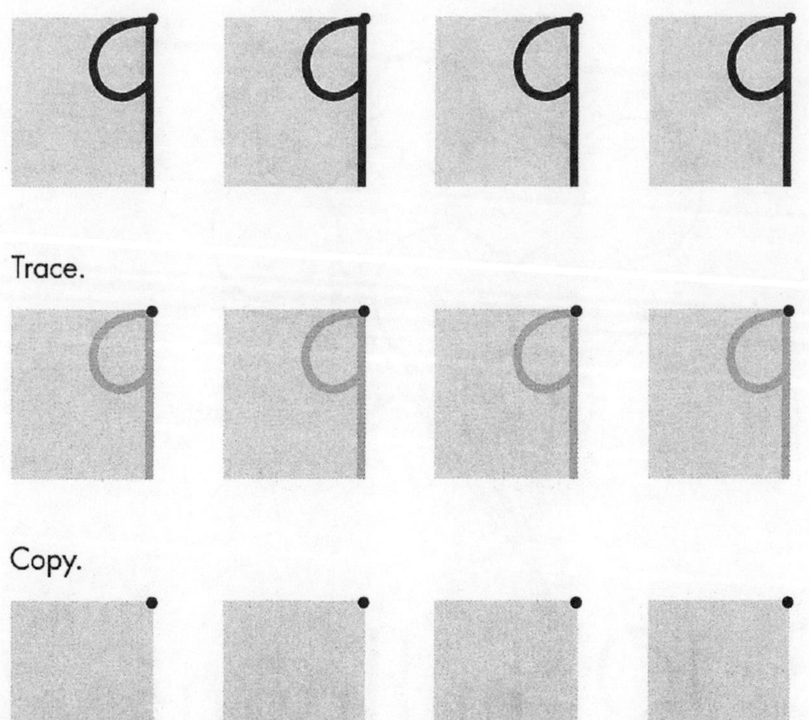

9 bees

10

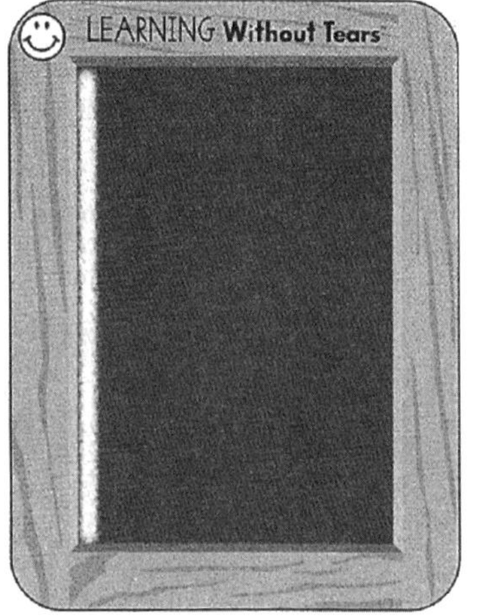

BIG LINE

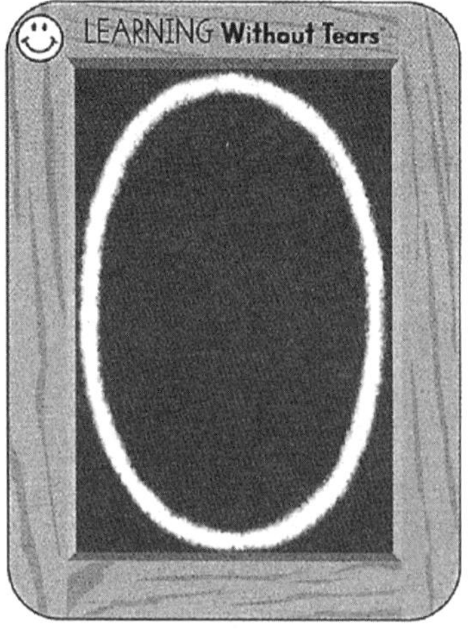

BIG CURVE
+ GO AROUND

ten

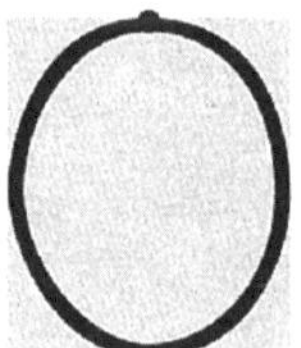

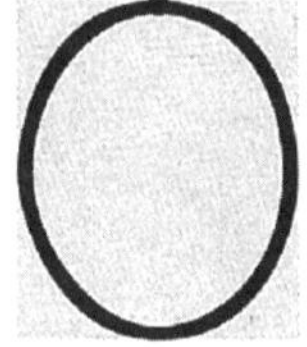

Trace.

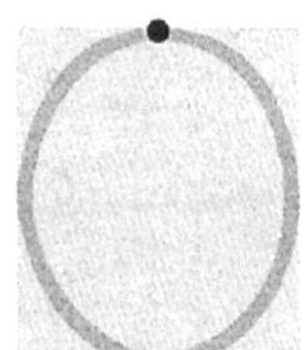

Copy.

10 balloons

Numbers for Me

I can write 1 to 10.

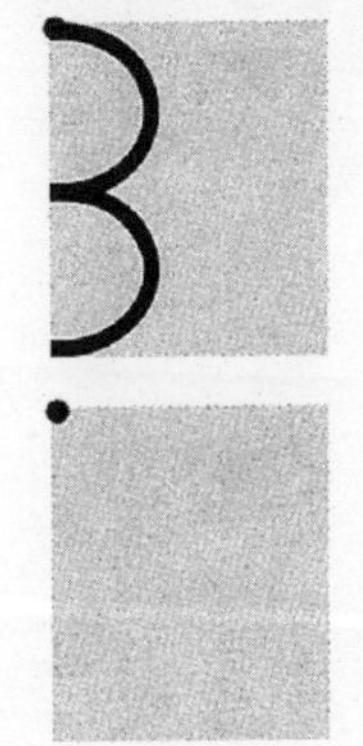

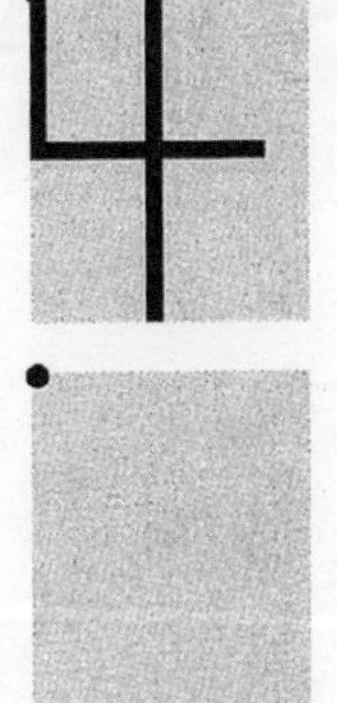

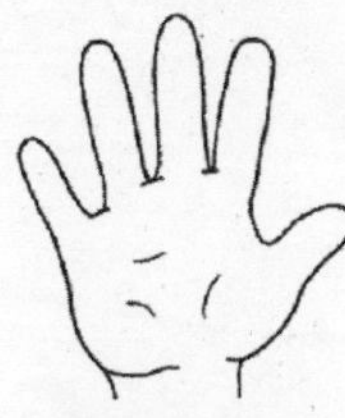

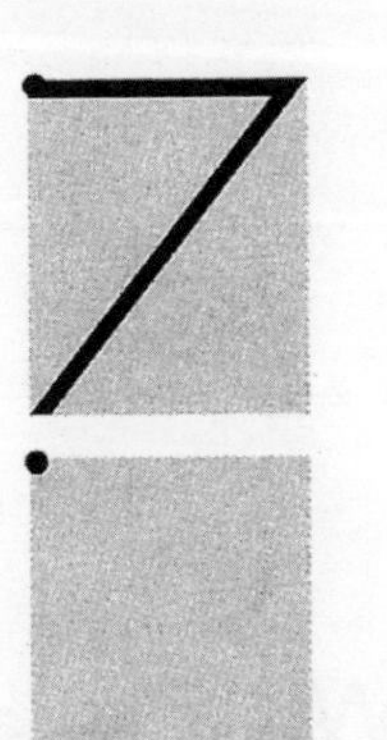

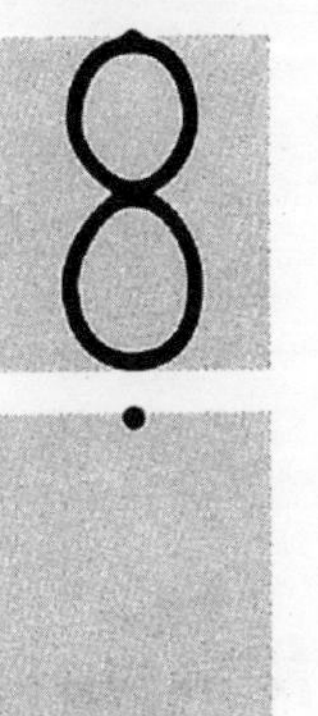

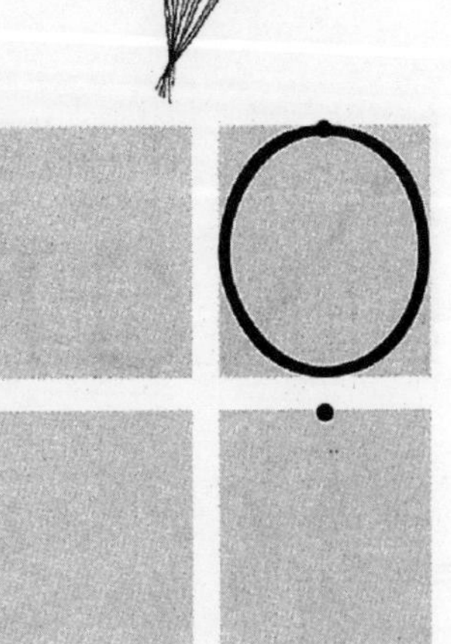

Teacher demonstrates.
Child copies below.

Completed *Kick Start Kindergarten*! Way to go!